KU-507-604

For permission requests, write to the author,
addressed "Attn: Permissions Required,"
at the address below.

TheNewKitchenTableBook@gmail.com

First Edition

ISBN: **9798321826652**

Author's Name: **Amit Gupta**

Title: **The New Kitchen Table**

Disclaimer

This book, including all its content, is for informational purposes only and does not constitute professional advice of any kind. The views expressed are solely those of the author and should not be interpreted as expert instruction or commands. While every effort has been made to ensure the accuracy of the information presented herein, the author and publisher do not assume and hereby disclaim any liability to any party for any loss, damage, or disruption caused by errors or omissions, whether such errors or omissions result from negligence, accident, or any other cause.

This work is intended to provide helpful and informative material on the subjects discussed. It is sold with the understanding that the author and publisher are not engaged in rendering medical, health, psychological, legal, financial, or other professional services. If the reader requires personal assistance or advice, a competent professional should be consulted.

The author and publisher specifically disclaim any responsibility for any liability, loss, or risk, personal or otherwise, which is incurred as a consequence, directly or indirectly, of the use and application of any of the contents of this book.

Some names and identifying details have been changed to protect the privacy of individuals unless expressly stated otherwise. Any resemblance to actual persons, living or dead, or actual events is purely coincidental.

"Growth Is The Art Of Questioning Answers"

The New Kitchen Table

DIPOLE IS THE PURPOSE OF NOYA

By
Amit Gupta

FOREWORD

Your New Growth

For generations, fireside chats with friends have been the setting for informal yet significant conversations, leaving us with valuable lessons. Similarly, a sacred space within our home has served the same purpose. This cherished space is our 'Kitchen Table,' a family dialogue and bonding foundation. My book "The New Kitchen Table" pushes you to understand how this simple tradition of gathering around the kitchen table can strengthen family ties and encourage open conversations. I have compiled some of my family discussions between myself (Amit), my wife (Nidhi), and our son (Ishu), which have been held around our kitchen table over the years. In this book, I have explored how Ishu's endless questions from our answers contributed to our family's collective growth.

"Growth is the Art of Questioning Answers."

In Search Of The Answers

Your sole purpose should be learning and developing life skills to prepare you for future events. A crucial gap to achieve this is proactive self-discovery of essential life skills. **'The New Kitchen Table'** seeks to bridge this gap, providing early guidance on crucial real-life skills, thus enabling you to explore your fear-free future.

The Map For The Path Ahead

The kitchen table is not merely a physical space but a symbol of the informal learning experiences shared between family members. Here, each family member absorbs values, attitudes, and skills that shape their lives in multiple ways. Through relatable narratives and practical advice, I aim to equip you with the tools to shape your family discussions at the kitchen table. I am sure that with the suggested frameworks, you can find patterns in life's chaos.

The following statement summarises the entire book.

DIPOLE, PURPOSE, NEAT – OPTIMISM – YOGA – ADAPT

- The **DIPOLE Cycle** is a systematic approach to understanding and navigating life's events, comprising seven steps - Driver, Intake, Prepare, Outgrowth, Learn, Examine and Cycle.
- The **PURPOSE** Scale is an essential 21 end-to-end learning principles, broken down into three phases: Begin, Middle and End. It suggests a structured path for personal development, focusing on self-discovery and achieving meaningful learning goals.

  The **NEAT Relationship** is a conceptual model that differentiates between favourable (Anchor Tower) and opposing (Nemesis Tower) relationship dynamics. The focus is on the evolution from strangers to friends or enemies based on trust, enthusiasm (Elan), and Ego, governed by life events.

- The **OPTIMISM Matrix** guides your life's actions by evaluating and balancing Health, Money, Purpose, and Time.
- The **YOGA Framework** is a nine-step process evaluation method for identifying, understanding, and bridging life's gaps, leading to your best outgrowth.
- The **ADAPT Framework** outlines the money management learnings: Acquiring, Disbursing, Allocating, Preserving, and Tracking money for sustainable and balanced living.

I have written the stories in small and sizable chapters that are easy to follow. 'The New Kitchen Table' does not pretend to have all the answers. Instead, it will be like that friend who, while they can't fix car issues, will sit with you and laugh while you both wait for help. It would help if you viewed this book as a conversation starter and a companion for those moments when life feels like a puzzle, missing half the pieces. It will remind you that while you may not control the winds of change, you can adjust your sails, sometimes with some duct tape and little hope.

Each chapter, with its unique blend of stories, analogies, and practical tips, is designed to be a lantern in the fog of life. It is for those who have ever felt overwhelmed by the sheer scale of "adulting" and for those who have ever wondered, "Is it supposed to be this complicated?"

You Are Invited

So, join me, grab a cup of coffee or tea, and prepare to laugh, learn, and maybe even shed a tear or two. I welcome you to my family's fireside chat at 'The New Kitchen Table,' – where we share our life's greatest lessons and hope to make a little difference in your life. This invitation is for:

- Those blessed by life's gifts also recognise they've faced struggles closer than many.
- Those grandparents who cherish family time and eagerly await reunions, as do those fortunate to live with their loved ones daily.
- Individuals who cause mischief and find themselves in trouble.
- Exceptionally talented and ambitious kids, alongside those uncertain about their future post-education.
- Those families gather around their kitchen table regularly, and those who find such gatherings rare.
- Siblings who see the unique and special qualities in each other, even if unnoticed by others.
- Those individuals lucky enough to find their pillars of strength following the loss of a loved one and those currently journeying through grief.
- Those who have overcome life's low points have become a source of growth for others.
- Those optimists view life with a bright outlook, and those who struggle to find the light.
- And anyone who falls in between the above groups.

About the Author

I, **Amit Gupta**, warmly invite you to join me at my kitchen table, a place where I discuss the good, the bad, and everything in between moments with my family. With a BA[Hons] in Economics and master's degrees in both Computer Applications and Business Administration, I have spent decades navigating the complexities of data and technology in the corporate world. Yet, it is the invaluable time spent around my kitchen table that has truly defined me, providing extraordinary insights into my professional life and transforming chaos into clear, understandable lessons.

'The New Kitchen Table' marks my first step towards forming a lifelong trust with you, empowering you to shape your narratives as part of your kitchen table. This book offers more than a collection of stories; it serves as a gateway into my knowledge base, revealing the experiences that have given me extraordinary learning. From being an ordinary boy on the brink to leading a remarkable life, every event and every relationship has guided me through my challenges and equipped me to guide my son through his.

Acknowledgements

At the heart of this book lies the essence of countless interactions, shared moments, and the impacts of the relationships that have shaped me. To encapsulate my gratitude in a few words is a task far more challenging than writing **The New Kitchen Table** itself, yet it is a task I undertake with joy and pride.

To Ishu, my son, your endless curiosity and positive spirit have not only enriched my life but have also been the spark that ignited the creation of this book. Your laughter and curiosity have brought to light the depth and beauty of my everyday moments. Thank you for inspiring me to write this book and working with me tirelessly to make my dream come true.

Nidhi, my life partner, your support has been my stronghold and anchor. Your strength and grace bring immeasurable value to the family. Your insights and love have been the guiding light through my life journey, making this book as much yours as it is mine.

To my parents, who have instilled in me the values and resilience that form the cornerstone of my character, I owe an enduring debt of gratitude. Your sacrifices, love, and wisdom have shaped the person I am today. The foundation you provided has been my constant source of strength and inspiration.

To my sisters, in-laws, extended family, and friends, each of you have contributed to and enriched my life with your presence. Your encouragement, support, and shared moments have added layers of depth to my knowledge, which I have used to build every chapter of this book.

Thank you to my colleagues, who have been a source of encouragement and camaraderie. Our professional paths have offered me unique perspectives and insights, enriching my narrative and understanding of the world.

To the team at the local coffee shop, thank you for brightening my mornings with your smiles and excellent coffee for last few months.

Lastly, I extend my deepest gratitude to authors who have left a mark on my life, whether through personal interactions or the pages of their books. Your stories, experiences, and wisdom have touched me immeasurably and continuously shaped my life.

This book reflects all the love, lessons, and laughter shared along the way. I extend my heartfelt love and respect to my readers.

Dedicated to countless lives, we'll touch,
Binding us all through our stories, thus,
A tribute to bond and love, Ishu & Nidhi,
Your strength and grace are a guiding light to Infinity.

Table Of Stories

I

You Are All
Welcome At
'The New Kitchen Table.'

———————●———————

DIPOLE : Driver

Story 1

The Unspoken Storm

My home is usually lively, with my son Ishu's laughter and endless questions. We look forward to our daily dinner discussions at the kitchen table. Our discussion could be about relationships, sometimes fear, sometimes a sense of optimism and sometimes sadness about being unable to achieve what we meant to accomplish that day. Ishu has moved to a phase in life where, beyond physical growth, emotional and mental growth is critical. With the right kind of support from us to set up a strong foundation, he can show what he is capable of in the real world.

One day, as I stood in the kitchen cooking dinner, I saw it had turned into a beautiful evening. Our kitchen window faces west, and you can see the sunset casting a soft, warm yellow and orange light through the window. The kitchen smelled of curry cooking, a comforting blend of spices and flavours. It was one of those moments when I felt entirely in my element, feeling the genuine pleasures of my life. And I was thinking about the lovely moments of our recent Scotland trip.

The usual master chef of our home, my wife Nidhi, was due back from a long day at the nursery school and had assigned the task of preparing my special dish, fajita wraps, for her as it is her favourite Friday night dinner (of course, when we are not ordering take away). Do not get me wrong —I am no cooking genius, and it has never been my thing. I have always preferred enjoying food rather than cooking it. If you were to ask me about the significant changes I have made during these changing times, learning to cook would top the list, enabling my wife to dedicate herself fully to enriching the lives of little ones in her nursery.

While the cooking and Scotland trip occupied my mind, the peace was interrupted by a squeaky noise on our staircase made by the heavy footsteps of Ishu. He settled into a chair at the kitchen table, burying his head in his hands, the image of an overwhelmed young man wrestling with enormous personal expectations.

"I just do not know, Dad," his voice barely rose above a whisper, starkly contrasting with his usual loud and confident tone.

**"Unspoken storms ultimately
pass by our absolute inner strength."**

"Do not know what?" I asked, turning off the stove. My full attention was now directed towards him.

As a parent, there are occasions and events when you know you must be 100% in the present moment with your kids. I knew this was one of those moments.

"This... all of this. Am I good enough? Am I even cut out to be something in this life? I feel as if I have no energy left. I do not have any special talent to offer this world. I am sorry, Dad." His words tumbled out, each laced with doubt.

"You have always been more than enough. But why the sudden doubt?"

He looked up, his wet eyes mirroring the unspoken storm. "It is just so much, Dad. The competition, the pressure. I look at everyone else, and they all seem to have figured everything out."

I sat opposite him at the kitchen table and said by holding his hand. "Son, comparing yourself to others is like reading the middle of their book and not seeing the beginning of your own. Your path is yours alone, unique, and valuable."

"But what if I fail? What if all this leads nowhere? What about money, time, and sacrifices that you, Mum, and I are making?"

"Failure is not the enemy; fear of it is. As for money and time, consider them investments, not just in your career, but in discovering who you are and who you can become." I said.

He sighed, a mix of frustration and exhaustion. "I just

need some direction, Dad. Some sign that I am on the right path."

So, we were around the kitchen table, which became more than just a place to eat. It became a melting pot of my son's worries, hopes, and dreams. It was the right time for me to share some of my own experiences with him, like my wife and I had done many times before this day. But this chat had a different feeling. It was not just any other moment in our lives but a crucial stage in shaping a kind spirit. We were not just talking about exams here. It was about life's purpose. It was the time to pluck some leaves from my tree of life and tell him, "Everything is just fine and as it should be."

Story 2

I Am A Collection
Of My Stories

As the sunlight faded, Ishu and I remained seated at the kitchen table, ready to merge stories with the aromas of our evening meal.

"Dad, how did you manage all this?" he asked, his voice a blend of curiosity and a sombre tone.

I gave a gentle smile while grasping the weight of his question - "We all go through various events in our lives. Whether these events are small or life-changing, each one is a part of a story in itself and has the potential to become a bigger story. These events come together to shape us into the way we are today. A similar collection of stories has shaped me as well."

He leaned forward, intrigued. "How are you so confident that every event matters? You may not recall some, or some do not even mean anything. Some are life-changing, which I understand, but how can every event shape us? For example, how can today's chat be significant in our life."

"We are connected to those around us, creating a rich, shared human experience. Every laugh, every challenge, every dream, and every setback is a connected story in itself. Some events may seem trivial to you, but they may have a larger impact on the lives of others. Take, for example, our chat today at the kitchen table. It started as just a normal chat between father and son, but we do not know what impact it will have on you and maybe the future of others." I said.

He nodded unconvinced but with some expression of understanding in his eyes. He was trying to motivate me to explain a bit more.

> **"Our stories get life through some seen and some unseen connections."**

I reached across the table to hold his hand. "Ishu, the effort you put in today to build something of your own is not just about you alone. It is also about the countless lives you will be touching in future. You are not just writing your story; you're also contributing to mine, your mother's, and your friends just like I am doing for you. We all fit into each other's plans and journeys, impacting them in multiple ways. Our stories are interconnected, and we often do not realise this because we do not have the eyes to see the invisible connections that shape all of us. Who knows where all this will end, given that we have made a beginning."

"Ishu, sometimes our life for others is much like this kitchen table. It is straightforward and unassuming, but it's been the backdrop to countless stories. Right here, we exchange our tales, ambitions, and worries. But within every single event we share, whether they appear significant or trivial, there's a possibility of something incredible."

Notes

Story 3

Manifestation Of Miracles
In My Life

Here I was with an apron on, taking on the chef's role, while across from me, Ishu had no idea about a historical event we were about to discuss, because of which his existence, as a miracle, came about. I wished Nidhi was here to share her version of the miracle. But maybe that was too much to expect, given that she must be busy with her nursery kids.

Then, as I was about to start my side of the story, the usual kitchen boss, Nidhi, unexpectedly made the entrance earlier than expected, adding the perfect twist to our story of invisible connections. It was also a minor miracle of sorts for me. Little did he know, he was on the brink of discovering the spicy tale of how his parents met. It was shaping up to be an evening sprinkled with a dash of destiny, a pinch of past, and a good scoop of family secrets, ready to be served.

The New Kitchen Table

In my experience, if you start talking about different topics, the person under self-made stress gets calm. I could see the same happening to Ishu. My wife joined us, setting the stage for sharing a memorable and genuine chapter of our lives with him. It is a true story of how visible and invisible connections shaped our family. And do not laugh because those watching you in the café, on a train, at home, or on a bus might get infected by your laughter.

I looked at Ishu: "I wanted to get my marriage arranged, and my preference for an arranged marriage was not due to any shortcomings but simply because the right connection had not sparked yet. My parents' search for a suitable partner was proving to be ineffective. I started doubting my dad's social skills and my mom's connections. But that is how it was, and I could not accept things as they were. So, there I was, requesting my brother-in-law to advertise my matrimonial profile in the newspaper, like tossing a coin into a wishing pond, hoping the newspaper ad does not end up wrapping someone's samosas instead."

I turned towards Nidhi: "Here in the UK, I was grappling with my job, surviving on a tragic diet of my friends' cooking disasters—alternating between raw and charred. The alternative was a grim choice between suffering through my disastrous cooking attempts or surrendering to a monotonous life of pizza. Meanwhile, you are in Kolkata, likely queen of the kitchen, unaware of my grim situation."

Nidhi: "And there I was, completely unaware that my future husband was making waves in a newspaper I never read. I must say, it was quite the moment. My uncle, waiting at his friend's office, bored out of his mind, spotted your ad in the local newspaper. His excitement was felt by everyone on his phone call to my dad as if he had found a hidden gem."

Me: "My parents were at their wits' end, honestly. They tried everything. When they heard the newspaper ad did work, they could not believe it. I do not want to tell you what other kinds of calls both my brother-in-law and I were getting because of that single newspaper ad. I still laugh thinking about those strange calls."

Nidhi: "Following that initial spark, my parents and your dad's parents took the next logical step: they exchanged our profiles and photos, setting the stage for our first meeting."

Me: "The moment I saw your photo, the first thing that came out of me was, 'She's going to be my wife.' I still can't explain why, but I strongly felt you would be my life partner."

Me, looking at my wife with a smile: "And then your parents called the whole thing off? I was devastated. My grand romance had not started, and it was already over!"

Wife (with a playful, sarcastic raise of her eyebrows): "Yeah, my parents were unsure. But fate had other plans. (Her expression softens into a warm, loving smile) Something just told them to give you another chance."

Me: "and swiftly moving on to the day of our first date. I came prepared with gifts, confident that I will impress you."

Wife: "And I still recall you talking for 44 minutes straight, from job to girlfriends and everything under the sun. I counted! As usual, you never allowed anyone else to speak."

Me: "Hey, I was nervous and worried that you might change your mind just like your parents. And when I finally asked if you could cook, I do not know what I was thinking."

"Miracles are simply the right things happening to you at the right time and in the right way."

Wife: "I was shocked! But it was sweet in a weird way. And look at us now. Who would have thought a newspaper ad would lead us here?"

Me: "And yes, our worlds began to shift unexpectedly. Our families kicked off wedding planning like world leaders at a high-stakes summit, and all this pageantry unfolded in front of our own eyes. Two individuals, previously strangers from thousands of miles apart, connected solely through a modest newspaper ad, were suddenly on a path to meet, marry, and start a new life together in the UK. And then, Ishu, you entered our lives like a miracle, beginning a unique new story."

"So, Dad, you guys are saying I am here because of a newspaper ad and your cooking question to Mom on your first meet-up," he said.

We all laugh, thanks to his signature one-liner that never fails to deliver. He finally understood that the manifestation of miracles in our lives can often unfold in the most unexpected ways, shaping our paths and the essence of our being. He understood that my encounter with his mum, a pivotal chapter in our family life, exemplifies such miraculous turns. It was not just about finding love through coincidences but the unforeseen impacts that followed, leading to life-changing events like bringing him to this world.

Endnote Reflections

Miracles are not always grand or earth-shattering. Sometimes, they are simply the right things happening at the right time, like meeting someone who changes your life or a newspaper ad. These experiences remind us to stay open to possibilities, embrace the unexpected, and appreciate the interconnectedness of the impact of our choices. Bear in mind that miracles do happen, often in ways we least expect but exactly when we need them. Sometimes, your small step towards a path you have never experienced could make you the source of something great. It is as if that path is waiting for you to arrive and light it up for others to follow in the future. Those who understand this will enjoy every single moment in life because they know their actions will cause a wave for others to ride on, even if they do not.

Notes

Story 4

When The Universes Collide, Stars Are Born

A few hours had flown by, and I noticed a shift in Ishu's mood, a hint of optimism creeping in. I had laid out the idea that life's full of surprises; sometimes, the unexpected and innocent act can lead to a series of miracles. Sure, we hustle and sometimes do not understand the gravity of our actions, yet some things remain beyond our control and should remain like that. I reflected on my detours, like that leap of faith with the newspaper ad—a move none imagined would bring us to this day. It was the essential lesson I aimed to give him. I could tell he was piecing together this puzzle, seeing how his existence blended unforeseen paths—convinced that he was starting to understand that great results appear when various events align with the intention of genuine change, but we have to perform our act in that event. I noticed a calmness in his breathing and facial expressions because now he understands that his career choice depends not only on him but also on those who will experience his presence in the future. He has to play his part today, free from the fear of failure in future.

Our conversation wrapped up with that, and we enjoyed our fajitas, which tasted better than ever that night. Who could have imagined that a candid family discussion at our kitchen table would inspire a section of this book? Little did we know that the humble kitchen table in our home would become the title of this work and resonate with countless lives.

Endnote Reflections

"Growth is the Art of Questioning Answers."

We all bring something new into the world to change what exists or slightly tweak it to keep progressing. We should do our part and let whatever higher force give life to our act. It is not really up to us to animate our creations. Understanding this can help you find calling faster. Those who do not grasp this concept might find themselves constantly searching, wondering without direction, in a quest for meaning and purpose.

Motivating yourself can be challenging if you are not an active person. Understanding and acknowledging this can shift your perspective, turning uncertain acts into a stepping stone for growth and new ventures. These acts become stepping stones when your path crosses with others, creating new connections and opportunities for growth and change. Your actions today can reshape your future and impact those around you. Hence, do not weigh yourself with too many expectations or feel victimised; instead, focus on moving forward one step at a time. There is no perfect life, perfect act, or perfect planning. We must channel what we have with us today and remain hopeful that our steps will bring us closer to missing pieces. Dead ends or setbacks are sometimes signals to redirect us from paths which are not meant for us and should not stop us from moving sideways. Though we cannot choose our beginnings, we certainly have the power to shape our endings.

The points mentioned below have consistently proven effective for me.

- **Explore something new outside your comfort zone (Doing)**—Actively seek out and engage in new hobbies or activities that differ from your usual routine. This could be anything from learning a musical instrument to starting a blog, volunteering, or joining a club or sport. By stepping out of your comfort zone, you may discover new passions or potential new paths for self-development and development.

- **Yearn the power of reflection and journaling (Writing)**—Spend time each day or week to reflect on your experiences and feelings. Writing your thoughts can help you better understand your thoughts and emotions, recognise patterns, and clarify what truly matters to you. This habit can help you find areas where you seek to change or grow. I have rediscovered myself more by writing and compiling 'The New Kitchen Table' than by discussing these topics.

- **Engage in meaningful communication and build connections (Listening and Speaking)**—Reach out and connect with different people—family, friends, mentors, or even new acquaintances. Sharing ideas and experiences can open your eyes to different perspectives and opportunities. Engage in meaningful conversations, ask for advice, and be open to learning from others' journeys.

II

DIPOLE : Prepare

Story 5

Unboxing Of Emotions

In my teens, I experienced something extraordinary – from being one of the last in class rankings, I moved to the top. This experience was so strange that no one around me saw it coming. I did not blame them because the kid who used to negotiate with god to scrape a pass became the one everyone noticed. Floodgates of popularity and fame opened; everyone wanted to be my friend and wanted to understand the secret sauce behind my success. I had a lot of emotional rollercoasters and no one to guide me. It was tough for me. No one could tell me if there was a step-by-step guide to dealing with these emotions.

Skip ahead several years, and I see Ishu hitting the same emotional rollercoasters in his teens. It is a different generation, but it is the same puzzling story to solve. One weekend, I saw him sitting on our garden swing, listening to music, and continuously looking at one of the trees. I knew something was up, but I wanted to give him space to open up in his own time. It is crucial to extend a helping hand to someone, but timing is everything – it's like catching someone just before they fall off the edge but allowing them to steady themselves first with their efforts. I am not saying to leave them hanging; it is more about being there when they're ready to reach out.

A few days later, one Monday afternoon, he returned from school, dropped his bag angrily at the door, and ended up at the kitchen table. His unusual act told me something was troubling him; I gently asked, "Everything ok, Ishu?" He muttered, "Yes, Dad," but his eyes betrayed him. So, I probed again, "What happened?" Predictably, as all teenagers do, he responded with a dismissive "Nothing." But after a few minutes, taking a few deep breaths to steady himself, he admitted, "I need some help from you to deal with my emotions." I realised it was time to hold his hand because I saw him near the cliff edge. I was unsure what was troubling him, but I was ready to offer him guidance to deal with the emotional challenge.

Use of the **DIPOLE Cycle** was the guidance I offered to him, and I hope it provides some direction in navigating your emotional challenges, the good, the bad, and everything in between. It is all about giving a real-life look at how someone ordinary, like me, experiences and navigates their feelings. I am no neurology expert so I will spare you the scientific jargon about brain functions. I would rather keep you engaged than induce sleep while you're reading my book.

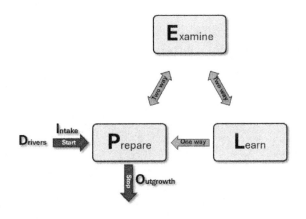

5.1 DIPOLE Cycle

Drivers, Intake, Prepare, Outgrowth, Learn, Examine

I will share my unique method for navigating life's complexities, including emotional challenges. The **'DIPOLE Cycle'** is an acronym for its components: Driver, Intake, Prepare, Outgrowth, Learn, Examine and Cycle. The DIPOLE Cycle is a conceptual framework I crafted to assist me in manoeuvring through various life events. By dissecting situations into distinct components, this model guides me in identifying and modifying specific aspects, enabling me to address the challenges effectively. Its seven interconnected parts outline a systematic approach to understanding and managing responses leading to positive outgrowth.

In the DIPOLE Cycle, three essential steps—Prepare, Examine and Learn initiated by Drivers and form the core of the process. The four core elements exchange information, internally and externally, through Intakes and Outgrowths. To clarify each component, I will use the example of preparing a familiar dish, an activity you already know and have experience with. After understanding the cycle's fundamentals, we will explore emotional experiences through the DIPOLE framework.

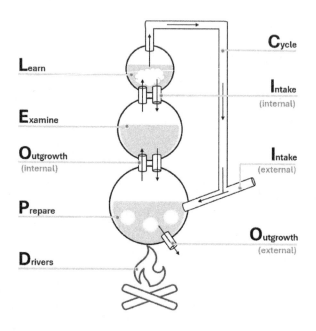

5.2 The Complete DIPOLE Cycle

DRIVERS are the underlying motives or reasons that initiate the cycle. They are the catalysts or independent events that set the entire cycle in motion. They are like a stove in your kitchen, helping you cook your dish.

PREPARE is where you lay the essential groundwork, where internal and external intakes are carefully considered and acted upon to achieve the intended growth. It can serve as the vessel on your stove, where the different ingredients of a dish are blended, guided by the knowledge of the recipe you trust and the cooking experience you have gathered.

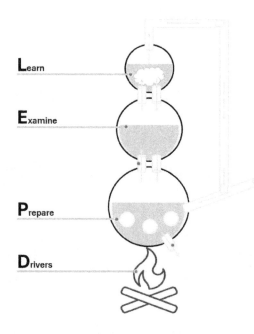

5.3 DIPOLE Cycle - Core

EXAMINE is an analytical step of the DIPOLE cycle that involves rigorously evaluating various steps within the PREPARE stages, blending insights from the LEARN stage based on past experiences. Here, one identifies feasible solutions to any discrepancies in the PREPARE workflow. Furthermore, new lessons are catalogued and returned to LEARN for future iterations. For example, you taste your dish at various stages of its preparation to identify any discrepancies. It involves comparing it to previous attempts, determining whether current preparation exceeds them or needs additional refinement. Identifying the gap allows the rectification of new errors to improve the dish. It helps you engage with your dish during preparation while allowing your mind to absorb new insights.

LEARN in the DIPOLE cycle compiles, reflects, and stores the insights gained from the EXAMINE stage, integrating these experiences into the current cycle or channelling them as vital intakes for the future. LEARN is where you harvest wisdom, ensuring readiness for future challenges. New insights are carefully noted throughout dish preparation, enriching the knowledge repository (LEARN) for the future.

Intake & Outgrowth (internal) is the pipeline through which internal results transition and interactions happen between the cores of the DIPOLE Cycle. It represents your internal dialogue while cooking your dish. It involves recalling and applying your experiences to complete the process.

Intake (external) refers to the input of external factors, such as interpersonal interactions, which serve as vital resources and inputs for the cycle. These represent the ingredients you gathered to create your dish, possibly a new recipe to experiment with something new in your kitchen.

Outgrowth (external) is tangible or observable growth from completing the DIPOLE cycle. In our example, this is the finished dish.

The **Cycle** represents the ongoing and iterative process of moving through the DIPOLE steps, highlighting that this is a continuous growth journey. For example, your expertise grows as you repeatedly prepare the same dish, transforming you into a master of that particular recipe through constant iterative practice cycles. Then, you use your new knowledge and insights to improve other cooking areas.

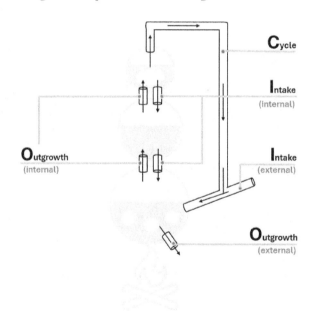

5.4 DIPOLE Cycle - Support System

Understanding Emotions Through DIPOLE Cycle

Now that we have laid the foundation for each component of the DIPOLE Cycle, let's explore the unboxing of our emotions. Let's look at them through the lens of my provided framework. I will guide you slowly through these steps and offer advice that might kickstart your handling of emotions effectively.

Let us assume that an external event occurs, which becomes a DRIVER for your emotional journey. PREPARE helps you absorb the intake from this event. There are two types of Intakes you get: External stimuli and Internal stimuli. External stimuli could be behaviours of others in this event, such as a compliment, an insult, a threat, or a fear. Internal stimuli delivered from LEARN could be your thoughts, memories, bodily sensations, or interpretations of events happening around you based on personal experiences, such as recalling the outcome of a past event.

The PREPARE takes these initial inputs and progresses them through one or more phases. After each step in the workflow, you share the results with the EXAMINE for detailed analysis. EXAMINE then identifies any discrepancies with the help of LEARN and then provides the final result to PREPARE, ensuring you refine each step before external outgrowth. These results can vary widely, from increased heart rate to hormonal changes and alterations in facial expressions to shifts in body language. These outgrowths can then serve as catalysts, propelling you into the next iteration of the DIPOLE Cycle. So, alterations in any step at any stage in the cycle can change the final outgrowth positively or negatively.

Enhancing PREPARE through EXAMINE and LEARN

When an event occurs, we instinctively engage ourselves

to interpret its significance to us and start to determine our appropriate reaction. Nevertheless, by training ourselves to step back and examine the situation from a detached perspective, as though we are spectators rather than participants in an event, we can provide a more measured and regulated response to the stimuli we receive. For instance, if a student fails and internally critiques with a generalised thought of, "I am not smart," might end up feeling significantly disheartened. But reframing their thoughts to, "That exam did not go as planned. What lessons can I learn from this experience to perform better next time? Is there someone who can offer me additional assistance in examining my situation?" could instigate feelings of optimism or motivation. This internal discussion can fundamentally alter your emotional landscape. Therefore, by adjusting your perspective, viewing obstacles as opportunities rather than setbacks, concentrating on the aspects within your control rather than those beyond it, or simply allowing yourself some leniency, you can effectively modify your emotional state. This strategy involves retraining your mind to follow a more constructive and supportive path. Below are some strategies that I have personally assessed over the years and found effective:

How you converse with yourself and perceive events can impact your emotional state.

- Recognizing your thoughts and feelings allows you to observe them without judgment. It can help you overcome automatic adverse reactions and choose a more balanced emotional response.

- Relaxation methods like deep breathing can reduce stress and anxiety, leading to a calmer emotional state.
- Instead of dwelling on the problem, focusing on finding solutions and acting on them can change the feeling of helplessness into a sense of control and determination.

Adjusting To Handle Intakes

How to change External Stimuli?

- Changing your surroundings, such as moving from a cluttered, noisy space to a calm, serene setting, can shift emotions away from stressful outcomes.
- Engaging in positive social interactions or distancing yourself from negative influences can improve mood and reduce stress.
- Switching from consuming harmful, distressing content to uplifting material can enhance feelings of happiness and reduce anxiety.
- Exercise, nutrition, and adequate sleep can boost mood and energy levels, reducing signals of lethargy or sadness to the brain.

How to change Internal Stimuli?

- Transforming negative thought patterns into positive affirmations through practices can alleviate negative feelings and increase self-esteem.
- Practising mind-calming techniques can help you become more aware of your internal states, allowing you to recognise and manage your emotions more effectively.
- You can train yourself to view challenging situations as an

opportunity to learn, leading to a feeling of empowerment rather than fear.

Adjusting To Handle Outgrowth

Dealing with the results of your emotional process is crucial, mainly because these reactions can loop back and influence your future emotional state. Understanding and managing the following aspects can help break potential cycles and lead to healthier emotional processing:

- Acknowledge your feelings without judgment. Feeling happy, sad, angry, or scared is perfectly normal.
- Express your feelings within a secure setting, such as talking to a reliable friend or penning your thoughts in a diary.
- Give yourself a moment to think before reacting to your emotions immediately.
- Communicate your feelings clearly and respectfully to others. Be aware of how your body language and tone of voice convey your emotions to others.

I have explained this in-depth exploration to deepen your understanding and provide you with the resources to navigate and control emotions effectively. It marks a step in the continual journey of self-discovery and emotional education. Next, we will explore a universal emotion that touches everyone: **FEAR**.

Notes

Story 6

Float, Swim, Or Sink In Fear

Once, I recounted an extraordinary moment from my life at the kitchen table – a life-changing event during my final college years. I celebrated as the top student in my second year. In an unforeseen twist, I failed in my final year. Such a failure would be a considerable setback for any student, but it struck me with overwhelming shock as I was accustomed to being at the top. In India, culturally, people often view educational success as the sole pathway to a better life; failing was more than a personal blow; it felt like societal condemnation. This failure was not just about repeating a year; it had real consequences. It blocked me from entering top MBA programs that year despite appearing in their entrance exams. It was not just a hiccup in my academic journey but a derailment of my future.

The New Kitchen Table

I needed to closely observe and change external and internal stimuli to address my fears of an uncertain future. I realised there were three distinct inputs I could give myself. The first option was to 'float.' It did not mean giving up; instead, it was about allowing myself a moment to breathe, not actively resisting the overwhelming tide of fear. By floating, I allowed myself to reflect and regroup emotionally and mentally. This approach was about seeking clarity and peace in the chaos to prepare for future actions with a calmer, more centred mind.

The second was to 'swim': to tackle my fears directly, to counteract the creeping doubts and the uncertainty that threatened to hold me back. This approach was about action — facing challenges head-on rather than allowing fear to dictate my path.

Lastly, there was the option to 'sink,' essentially surrendering to my fears, allowing them to dictate my life's direction. It was the easiest route in the short term but the most detrimental in the long run. Sinking meant succumbing to despair, forfeiting hope, and letting the weight of my circumstances drag me down into a state of inaction and defeat.

Facing widespread doubts from family and friends, I felt increasingly isolated, as if backed into a corner with everyone expecting the worst. The sense of isolation, compounded by doubt from others, was disheartening and demotivating. Yet, this difficult period taught me the crucial lesson of self-belief by applying my straightforward

DIPOLE Cycle. I altered the intake directed towards me, significantly changing my perspective on the situation. I understood this situation was uniquely mine, and seeking others' approval was unnecessary. I needed to recognise that relying on my inner strength and grit to steer through the scepticism was the appropriate action to take at that moment.

During the initial phase of addressing my emotional turmoil, I did not take any decision lightly. Overcoming my fears of exam phobias and converting failure into a catalyst for personal development was essential. I began by embracing education and skill updates during the gap year. I progressively started developing my knowledge and confidence in the field of computers.

> **"Your perspective is the lens through which your strength is either magnified or diminished."**

Repeating a year in college was a significant setback, yet I reframed it as an invaluable second chance at refining my understanding of my core subject, myself, and my emotions. I started an unpaid job the same year, pushing me to the limits; nevertheless, it provided me with essential hands-on experience and real-world experience. For me, standing still and 'sinking' was never an option. Every action I took, from academics to professional experiences, was a calculated step forward, each contributing to a more extensive journey of progress and self-improvement, all due to the change in my perspective on my circumstances and providing my brain with alternative methods to process my situation.

Recognising that you often unearth your true strengths in these moments of solitude is crucial. I understood the art of converting cynicism into a driving force, focusing not on persuading others but acting on my strengths. This shift in perspective enabled my brain to interpret situations positively, resulting in positive actions and emotions. You do not have to be truly alone in facing such challenges, but the ability to alter your story rests within you. Thinking that success and failure are just a perspective and that we only add value to every event to the best of our ability is the essence of self-development and overcoming adversity.

Story 7

I Added Value;
Success Or Failure
Was Just Opinion

In processing the failure in my college year, a life-changing moment, I realised the necessity of reframing my failure in a new light. It was not just a setback for me; it was a unique, once-in-a-lifetime learning opportunity that few have experienced. I understood that success and failure are largely matters of perspective, shaped by our beliefs and those of the people around us. What constitutes failure for one might be considered a success by another.

Confronted with my situation in the final year, I faced a choice: deep in self-pity, blaming fate and others for my misfortune, or see this as a golden opportunity to push my limits, to learn, and to find new opportunities for myself, especially since I had nothing left to lose. I opted for the latter, deciding to triple my efforts, demonstrate resilience, and keep moving forward. I embraced the concept that life's experiences, whether good or bad, contribute to my personal development. At that time, every event was an opportunity to enhance my value. I focused on learning and dismissed the binary labels of success and failure, recognising them as constructs that feed the ego.

By adopting a mindset centred on adding value and equipping myself with the necessary tools to navigate life's challenges, I prepared myself for continued personal evolution. I live by the mantra, "Growth is the art of questioning answers." Whether these answers are affirming or challenging, each one offers a chance to question myself and learn new lessons for future growth.

"Life will not necessarily get more comfortable in the future, but we can become more robust, adaptable, and better equipped."

It also implies that you should take risks without fearing failure but never have this misconception that misfortune will strike only once. Life consistently presents challenges in numerous forms, and failure, much like success, will find various ways to manifest at your doorstep. Even with every precaution taken to avert failure, you will inevitably face both fear and failure. Hence, it is crucial to learn to coexist with these experiences, work through them to add value to life, and continue to grow. Sometimes, you may need to travel the

I Added Value; Success Or Failure Was Just Opinion

same path again to absorb lessons fully and become better at dealing with those paths. In doing so, you not only conquer your emotional waves but also equip yourself to guide others through their detours in similar situations in future.

<u>Endnote Reflections</u>

Avoid the trap of thinking, "If this is my fate, then it must dictate my destiny." One event does not define your entire future. Often, we let a single negative experience cloud our judgment, leading us to believe that our destiny is bleak and will only mirror that unfortunate incident. However, it's crucial to remember that our path is shaped by a series of events and choices, not just one. We must not generalise our destiny based on a solitary setback but recognise that every step, good or bad, is part of a more extensive journey that is ours to steer toward a hopeful future.

Notes

Story 8

Travelling The
Failed Road Again

Confronting the fear of failure isn't a one-time event; it often requires facing it repeatedly. Each time, you will discover something new, reaching a point where the consequences of a failed attempt start to lose their sting. The cycle of perceiving failure negatively, which influences your mindset, begins to break. And you become more assertive in dealing with the emotional response of dealing with it. This approach takes perseverance, but having navigated through various failures myself, facing my fears cultivated character enhancement — a transformation visibly noticed by those around me.

After I passed my final year, I did not stop there. I signed up for the inaugural batch of internet-based distance learning programs for a Master in Computer Application (MCA) in India, a real challenge in the late '90s when internet access was limited and painfully slow. Juggling with distance learning, an unpaid full-time job, and two other classroom-based courses pushed my boundaries. Despite the odds, I succeeded in completing my MCA, a feat considering the low pass rate, which I estimate was between 3-5% nationwide.

"Nudge yourself daily; you will be miles ahead in a few years."

I aimed even higher and later enrolled in a new distance learning worldwide MBA program at one of the UK's top institutions while working full-time at an investment bank, a dream crushed due to my college final year failure. I pushed myself by choosing finance-heavy electives despite my engineering background. This period was challenging as I had just gotten married, we were expecting a baby, my father underwent major heart surgery, and we faced financial difficulties amidst the great recession in the UK. Confronting these challenges taught me to repeatedly walk the path confidently, each time more aware and resilient, proving that fear eventually loses its grip. I applied this lesson again when facing job losses, transforming each employment setback into an opportunity for higher pay, better positions, and valuable breaks to spend time with my family and pursue personal passions like writing.

I have shared this learning with my friends, and the ones

who took it to heart have seen incredible changes and growth. Sure, dozens of people have witnessed my journey and its ups and downs, but only a brave few decided to follow. It was not a walk in the park for them as well; it was tough. But now, they stand in a much better spot, much like I do, far ahead of where we all began. There is so much more to all this than I could ever squeeze into a few chapters. But for now, I hope what I am saying comes through clearly and helps you step forward positively towards your purpose in life, i.e. 'to learn'.

Notes

III

DIPOLE : Learn

Story 9

The Mountain Peak
Of Learning Named
PURPOSE

L et us proceed with the subsequent phase of the DIPOLE cycle, focusing on the LEARN component. Understanding its significance and function within the DIPOLE framework is crucial, as this will simplify and enhance our work with the EXAMINE stage later on. By grasping LEARN's essence, we unlock a smoother transition and comprehension of the entire cycle.

Ishu loves golf and school equally, but when it came to his Year 11 GCSEs in the UK—a significant set of external exams—he felt the heat. He had to tackle many other subjects besides the core stuff like maths and science. While he aced maths and science, he only hit average scores in the rest. This lack of focus led him to question me, "Dad, what is the purpose of learning these other subjects if I am all in on maths and science?" A similar question haunts our minds daily: Why must we learn so many new things if we only ever use a handful of them?

Each subject or event holds its unique value and imparts different learnings and tools, each pertinent at various stages of life. I hope my explanation of LEARN helps you carve out your learning journey. If it does, that would be fantastic! If not, it might point you towards finding your unique way of learning. Once its importance in the DIPOLE Cycle is understood, the path to take meaningful action to gain knowledge becomes significantly straightforward.

Comprehending the learning methods shapes how we approach life, making this understanding crucial for deeper self-awareness. It involves dissecting our psyche's 'operating system' across varying life scenarios to uncover the 'how' and 'why' of our reactions and decisions. Without insight into our internal mechanisms, we wander through life clouded by confusion and devoid of clear direction. Clarifying how we assimilate information and experiences is essential for informed decision-making. That is why LEARN is one of the core steps in the DIPOLE Cycle, enhancing our actions and facilitating our development. Consequently, for some, it guides their choices and paths.

> **"Learning fuels our life,**
> **and PURPOSE**
> **brightens its path."**

Focus On LEARN

In streamlining the LEARN stage, I crafted the acronym PURPOSE, each letter symbolising distinct attributes or values that play pivotal roles at various learning junctures from beginning, middle and end. The PURPOSE Scale offers a structured framework to navigate the multiple stages of learning throughout our lives, capturing seven specific themes in every stage, one for each letter of PURPOSE, making 21 attributes in total.

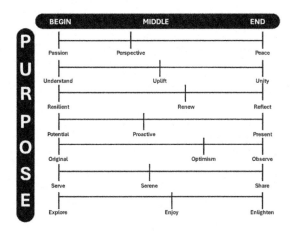

9.1 PURPOSE Scale

For example, some may begin their learning journey by focusing on 'Passion' (Begin - P) and aspiring towards 'Peace' (End – P) as their ultimate goal, thus traversing horizontally across the scale via 'Perspective' (Middle – P). Conversely, others may initially seek' Perspective', only to uncover their true 'Passion' at the end of the PURPOSE scale. This educational path is neither linear nor uniform for all; you can uniquely tailor your journey.

The New Kitchen Table

The critical takeaway is cultivating Passion, Perspective, and Peace within you. It is possible to have a strong passion but lack inner peace when young. This imbalance calls for a change in perspective, ensuring that you feel content and at peace with your life choices by the time you reach your full potential.

Consider all the letters in the PURPOSE acronym to construct your learning model from your life events. This approach helps you to continuously seek and refine yourself as you move through different phases of life, Begin-Middle-End. This scale is the easiest way to pinpoint what drives you at each stage of learning. As a dad, I have been guiding Ishu in figuring out his learning PURPOSE the way I have done mine. Once you identify your accurate scale, it can be your daily motivator, pushing you forward.

How can you bring this scale to life as a guide to discovering what you want to Learn? It is more like introspection, which entails posing crucial questions in response to life's events, understanding the answers provided by these occurrences, beginning with who, what, where, when, why, and how, collectively referred to by me as 'WISH' (popularly called 5W and 1H). These questions can teach valuable lessons about who you are and what you want from that situation. By pondering on WISH, you will be on a path of self-discovery. You gain clarity about your values, direction for your future, and a deeper understanding of what truly matters to you. This reflective process enables you to make decisions that resonate with your true self.

The Mountain Peak Of Learning Named PURPOSE

As we progress, each chapter will cover one attribute of the learning scale: PURPOSE, first covering seven attributes of Begin followed by seven of Middle and seven from End. By dissecting the intricacies of these 21 attributes, you will uncover the nature of self-development and self-discovery. Through endnote reflections, real-life examples, and actionable advice, I aim to convert theory into practice, guiding you step by step toward a more fulfilled and purpose-driven life.

Notes

Story 10

Art Of Being Animal

Every living organism, from humans to plants to animals, operates under specific rules, either self-imposed or externally imposed. Take a lion, for instance. In the wild, its task is to hunt, and the lion approaches this task with unmatched passion, mastering the art of hunting without concern for repercussions – no fears of jail time or handcuffs, legal challenges, or a boss to report to. They are all about the chase, with varying degrees of success governed by their rules, but inner fire drives their natural passion for hunting.

The story of the same lion in the circus is different altogether. Here, the lion has a 'boss'. This lion is not chasing his passion; he is performing tricks, a job far removed from his natural inclinations, to secure his daily meat ration. It involves adjusting to a new set of rules established by species far less skilled in hunting than lions. You can see that the contrast is stark when compared to his wild cousins. Our circus lion has yet to taste the thrill of the hunt. He has buried instincts, but not dead, clouded by an existence that caters more to the entertainment of different species than to the call of the wild.

But what can a caged lion do to rediscover his passion for hunting? He is not equipped with a library card, Netflix, or YouTube to ignite his lost love for the hunt, nor can he easily swap circus lights for the moonlit plains for his calling. To find his true calling, the lion needs a breakthrough, a return to nature, a leap back to the roots of his existence. He must collaborate with his kin, unlearn, and learn again to navigate the wild once more and reignite the passion for hunting within him despite the golden handcuffs of circus life. It involves breaking free from the expectations of others which do not belong to him. Only by breaking free from the constraints of his daily circus life can he rediscover his true passion.

So, what does it mean to live with your passion once you have discovered it? It is like breaking free from Earth's gravitational pull and venturing into space. It is free from everything which is holding you back. But in this journey, you carry what is essential – minimal baggage, leaving terrestrial constraints behind. Because in space, the only necessity for you will be sufficient fuel to maintain your flow and health, allowing you to pursue your desires uninfluenced by others. And on your journey, external opinions become irrelevant; after all, not everyone has the privilege of experiencing this unique freedom to be in space.

When you are living with passion, it's as if every cell of your body points in one direction, like atoms in iron point in one direction to make it a magnet or when your favourite song comes on, and every cell of your body can't help but move with the music. Your body, thoughts, and spirit are all in a 'flow' state, making you feel fabulous in a way that is hard to explain but amazing to experience.

People often compare passion to discovering a 'killer instinct.' I think it is more about awakening your true 'survival instinct' because living without your passion is like walking around with a soul trapped in a lifeless body, a heart that's stopped beating inside a body as good as a wooden coffin. You can find passion in anything, from what you do for fun to what you do for work or even the causes you believe in. Passion kicks in when you do things that feel right; they feel like they're part of your meaning in life. The beauty of us mortals is that we can find our passion, no matter what stage of life we are in, where we come from, or what jobs we do. It is all about getting involved, committing to something, and being driven by it.

Endnote Reflections

How do you find where your passion is? I suggest you try different things to see what motivates you. Sometimes, you will commence on an undiscovered path, but your passion could be the one to bring it to life. You may have to detour on roads never travelled by anyone to find such paths. It will bring you to your natural habitat and make you unbeatable, like the lion. So, mix the lion's instinct with the astronaut's freedom in space, and you will have a good recipe for finding and living your passion. No spacesuits or jungles are required, just the courage to hunt down what makes you come alive.

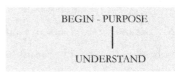
Story 11

I Am No Saint,
But I Can Listen

In this life, each of us has to deal with one or more challenges related to health, finances, or simply the lack of time to pursue what we love. But one thing is confirmed. We all want a listening ear for our troubles. Yet, we are reluctant to offer the same in return. And even if we do, instead of genuinely hearing others, we often fall into the trap of comparing our struggles to theirs, occasionally concealing our sense of relief that our situations are not as dire.

**"Holding on to struggles close
to you does little good;
conversely, sharing them
can be liberating."**

The New Kitchen Table

My parents are old and live far away, a whole day's travel from the UK. They only see the rest of my family and me once a year. Since moving to the UK, I have not skipped a day without calling them. Keeping in touch with them daily helps lift some of their worries and lets me chip away at my duties as their child. The only thing they are always looking for from me is regular communication and someone who listens to and understands their needs. So, just listening to them once a day makes long-distance living more manageable for us.

I am sure you have probably heard the saying about why we have two ears, two eyes, and only one mouth. It reminds us to listen and observe more but talk less. It helps in the professional world as well. As a technology consultant, I listen to what clients are struggling with. Often, they work out their solutions just by talking it through. Sometimes, they see me as someone they can trust to explain and solve their problems. So, understanding people by actively listening to them works in both a personal and professional setting.

Endnote Reflections

Here is how to get better at listening:

- Let people finish talking about what is on their mind, whether they're upset, excited, or anything else. Cutting them off is a no-go.
- Be there with them physically, mentally, and emotionally. People can tell when you are zoning out—it's all in your eyes and tone of voice.

- If you do not understand someone's problem, it is ok to say so. Or better yet, point in the direction of someone you know can help.

- Do not generalise or jump to conclusions based on your experience. I learnt this the hard way during a team activity once. We were assigned a quiz, and I dove in without reading the instructions correctly. I was struggling big time, while others seemed chill. It turns out that the last instruction said we were not supposed to solve anything – we just had to read the text.

Notes

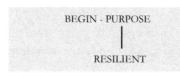
Story 12

You Are Cornered; You Are At The Turning Point

After reading the title, you might think this chapter is about some extreme survival story in my life. We all have enough of those experiences to fill pages, so I will not go there. Here is one of my experiences, which you may find hard to believe, but it's true.

It covers the first three years of Ishu's life with us. He had a speech delay; just to set the context, he did not say a word until after his third birthday, and his mode of communication was screaming and pointing. Once, while flying to India with his mom, his screaming was so intense that it delayed the flight by one hour. Yep, it is true; the crew had to bring in a doctor because they thought it was a medical emergency. There it was, my wife, trying her best to keep him quiet but stranded in chaos, surrounded by medical staff, crew, and impatient fellow passengers. For us, restaurants became a no-go zone; he could not manage sitting quietly. Our house was only silent from screams when he watched his favourite cartoon. It was like magic; he could sit there, completely absorbed for hours.

I was eager for him to call me 'papa,' and Nidhi was waiting for her first 'mummy.' We tried everything, from voice to hearing tests, but he did not speak. You might think, "Why did we not see a speech therapist?" Well, we tried. Getting an appointment was another story – they were hard to come by, and when we reached out, doctors informed us that it might just be a phase or timing issue. Ishu had his way of communicating, however. If he wanted something, he would grab our hand, lead us to the item, and point. Thirsty? He would drag us to the kitchen, point at a glass, then at the tap. It became our everyday communication style. But it did work; the only thing was that someone had to be with him all the time just in case he did not find anyone and started screaming again.

**"Facing a dead end feels
like everything is over.
Yet, stepping sideways might
reveal a new path awaiting discovery."**

I never lost hope, but Nidhi, who spent the most time with him, often found herself in tears, unable to decipher what was wrong with her son. Medical advice on Google suggested he might be in discomfort, but no medication

You Are Cornered; You Are At The Turning Point

seemed to make a difference. At times, when we tried to engage him, he would not even meet our eyes or give us a vacant stare, making us feel like strangers to him. We were both cornered.

Then, one day, he suddenly had a high fever. With conditions making it risky to take him out, we arranged for the GP to make a house visit. We braced ourselves, knowing the only update we could provide was that he had a fever. Upon the doctor's arrival, Ishu began his usual greetings with a lovely scream, which led the doctor to suspect he was in acute pain.

Trying to assess him further, the doctor asked, "Ishu, can you please show me your tummy?"

To our utter astonishment, he responded, "Yes," and lifted his T-shirt. Nidhi and I exchanged shocked glances. 'Yes' – that single word shattered the silence of years. Where did that come from? We had not heard him speak at all until that moment.

The doctor continued, "Do you have any pain?"

"No," he replied, with a smile forming on his lips.

A brief but astounding conversation between him and the doctor followed, consisting of 'yes' and 'no' answers, ending with him saying "Bye" as the doctor left.

That day, he marked a turning point, leaving us bewildered yet filled with a new glimmer of hope. By that point, we got cornered from every angle, and that short visit was a massive turning point in our lives. I have always prided myself on being a problem solver, feeling there was not something I couldn't piece together. Yet, I found myself utterly stumped by him. That significant day marked our startling revelation: he understood only English at the time, despite being surrounded by Hindi all the time. It might seem strange, but it is a fact. To this day, he mostly speaks English. Over the years, he has picked up more and more Hindi, but the mystery of how he favoured one language over the other remains unsolved. The only explanation we could think of was that his mom worked in a nursery school filled with English-speaking children during her pregnancy. Perhaps Ishu was attuned to these English-speaking kids' sounds, laughter, and screams even before he was born. That episode, that unexpected discovery during the GP's visit, was our turning point. If you have kids, maybe some of this sounds familiar. If not, consider this a sneak peek into potential future adventures of parenthood.

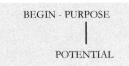
Story 13

Find An Anchor,
Not A Nemesis

We all aim to create meaningful relationships in our lives. Being a social creature, we sometimes find it hard to understand why some relationships last a lifetime while others fade away with time. We wonder why certain people become our support for life while others seem to pull us down. Also, knowing when to stay in a relationship and when to let go becomes complicated and confusing. Building a solid connection takes much work; you may destroy it by one event. We must also consider how much our ego affects these changes in relationships. To better understand all these dynamics, I developed Anchor and Nemesis Towers in the NEAT Relationships framework.

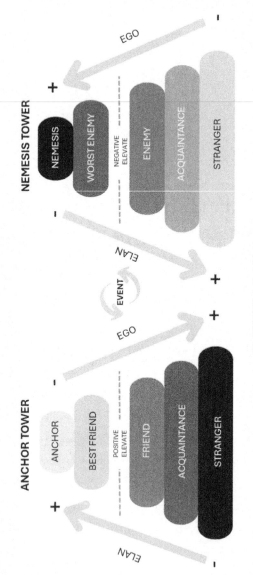

13.1 NEAT Relationships

Nemesis – **E** (Event, Elevate, Elan, Ego) – Anchor Tower

Find An Anchor, Not A Nemesis

NEAT Relationships

The **NEAT Relationships**, an acronym for **N**emesis – **E** (Event, Elan, Ego, Elevate) – **A**nchor **T**ower, is a conceptual framework for understanding the dynamics of human connections. It categorises relationships into two distinct pathways: the Anchor Tower, which represents the positive development of relationships, and the Nemesis Tower, which signifies the deterioration of social bonds. This model explores how relationships can evolve or regress through stages based on the impact of life events and fluctuating ego levels. Through this lens, the model aims to explain the complex nature of interactions and guide you in navigating your social environments more effectively. It is a tool designed to help you recognise the patterns and factors that strengthen or weaken your connections with others.

Elan and Ego

In the Anchor and Nemesis Tower, 'Elan' and 'Ego' play crucial roles in defining the nature of relationships.

Elan refers to your energy, enthusiasm, or the positive spirit you bring into your interactions with others. It is being open, trusting, and genuinely interested in others. In the context of these towers:

- In the Anchor Tower, high Elan moves you upward towards positive relationships like Best Friend and Anchor, symbolising growth in trust, connection, and mutual respect. These relationships involve building each other up and feeling more connected as Elan increases.

- In the Nemesis Tower, low Elan contributes to negative relationships. Ideally, balancing Elan influences interactions, but it might not be enough to nurture friendship in the context of rising Ego.

    Ego represents self-centeredness, pride, or the degree to which one's needs, desires, and perspectives dominate the relationship.

- In the Anchor Tower, a lower Ego is considered beneficial. It allows relationships to flourish into positive territories like Best Friend and Anchor, where mutual understanding and humility prevail over self-interest.
- In the Nemesis Tower, a high Ego, especially with lower Elan, escalates the relationship from mere Acquaintance to Enemy or even Nemesis. It indicates a progression towards hatred and conflict, driven by self-importance and lack of mutual respect.

From Stranger to Acquaintance and then Friend or Enemy

In the Anchor and Nemesis towers, our relationships with others evolve from strangers to acquaintances to friends or enemies. It all starts with two individuals being unknown to each other. That is the Stranger stage. Then, as you get to know a bit about each other, you move up to Acquaintance. Here, you have a basic grasp of who the other person is but are not close yet. The spark that ignites this fire is 'Trust.'

Things get interesting for both parties when the Ego and Elan play their part. Depending on how your Elan and

Find An Anchor, Not A Nemesis

Ego change, you may end by moving into Anchor or Nemesis Tower. Suppose you like the stranger and start with high Elan and low Ego. You move upwards in Anchor Tower, but then some event in your life lets' your ego overshadow the relationship, making your enthusiasm and trust (elan) dip. This event leads you to move away from friendship and drift towards considering them as your Enemy, climbing the Nemesis Tower. The more you focus on yourself and your ego and put less effort into building a strong bond, the less you want to be around them because you are now entirely concentrated on yourself.

Conversely, if Elan grows positive and you start putting your ego aside, you are headed for a stronger bond and climbing further up the Anchor Tower. You will want to hang out more and enjoy each other's company. The journey through these stages can unfold rapidly or gradually, depending on the time and effort both parties put into elevating to the next stage.

Thus, Elan and Ego are two sides of a tower in your relationships: balancing them leads to healthier, more positive connections (Anchor Tower), while letting Ego outweigh Elan can push relationships into negative connections (Nemesis Tower).

**"An anchor in life
multiplies positivity,
While a nemesis
divides all we cherish."**

Positive / Negative Elevate

'Elevate' in both towers represents moving to a higher level within the relationship dynamics. Still, the nature of this elevation differs based on whether it is in the context of the Anchor Tower or the Nemesis Tower.

- **Positive Elevate (Anchor Tower)** - 'Elevate' in Anchor Tower symbolises the enhancement and deepening of relationships. Relationships improve as trust and mutual respect (Elan) increase and self-centeredness (Ego) decreases. Moving from 'Friend' to 'Best Friend' and ultimately to 'Anchor' shows a positive elevation. The shared experiences become more enriching, bonds strengthen, and the connection becomes a supportive, anchoring force in each other's lives. 'Positive Elevate' is about rising through levels of friendship leading to mutual growth.

- **Negative Elevate (Nemesis Tower)** - 'Elevate' here is the escalation of negative aspects within a relationship. As animosity or resentment (negative Elan) grows and Ego becomes more prominent, the relationship deteriorates, moving from 'Enemy' to 'Worst Enemy' and finally to 'Nemesis.' Here, 'Negative Elevate' means intensifying negative feelings and conflicts, where the relationship becomes more strained and antagonistic, crossing the escape velocity where the other person becomes a significant adversarial force in your life. But suppose you do not invest enough energy and begin focusing on other relations in your life. These individuals will likely drift away from your life and eventually become part of an unhappy memory.

In summary, 'Elevate' in both towers signifies the progression or movement within the spectrum of relationships, either towards stronger, positive connections or more negative dynamics.

Best Friend to Anchor

In the Anchor Tower, moving from 'Best Friend' to 'Anchor' signifies a deepening of the relationship. A 'Best Friend' is someone with whom you share a close, personal bond, characterised by trust, enjoyment, and mutual support. It is someone you can rely on and share your thoughts with, someone who understands you well. Transitioning from 'Best Friend' to 'Anchor' means this relationship has become even more significant. An 'Anchor' is not just a best friend; they are a selfless foundational support in your life. They provide stability, guidance, and strength, especially during challenging times. They are a person you can lean on, who helps to keep you grounded, and whose presence is essential to your well-being. The progression from 'Friend' to 'Anchor' involves an increased level of trust, reliance, and depth of connection with nearly zero egos between each other.

Worst Enemy to Nemesis

In the Nemesis Tower, transitioning from 'Worst Enemy' to 'Nemesis' marks a significant shift in the dynamic of opposition or conflict. A 'Worst Enemy' represents a considerable personal challenge or threat, often involved in direct conflicts or competitive situations—a person whose actions or existence seems to counter your interests, causing frequent stress or confrontations. Moving from 'Worst Enemy' to 'Nemesis' signifies that this adversarial relationship has deepened beyond ordinary rivalry or dislike. A Nemesis's presence or actions seem destined to oppose your goals or values, representing a significant and possibly insurmountable dislike. The progression from 'Worst Enemy' to 'Nemesis' involves an escalation in the intensity and permanence of the conflict. It's a transition that often pushes you to your limits and requires significant effort to overcome. Avoid taking any relationship to this stage because it will destroy both parties.

A mathematical explanation to understand and unlock the full potential of your friendship, which can take you closer to your purpose in life, use the formula:

POSITIVE ELEVATE = ELAN / EGO

The larger the EGO (a lot of resistance or barriers), the more ELAN (effort, energy, trust) is needed to achieve ELEVATE in friendship. Conversely, reducing EGO requires less ELAN to achieve the same level of ELEVATE. It illustrates how balancing personal drive and humility can elevate your growth or the depth of a relationship.

NEGATIVE ELEVATE = EGO / ELAN

In this scenario, where Negative Elevate is the inverse of Positive Elevate, the larger the EGO (indicating higher levels of resistance or self-centred barriers), and the smaller the ELAN (indicative of less effort, energy, and trust), the greater the NEGATIVE ELEVATE in a relationship creating the condition for being a worst enemy. In other words, an increase in EGO and a decrease in ELAN result in a negative elevation in the relationship. It demonstrates that an imbalance dominated by ego and a lack of mutual effort can diminish the quality or lower the state of a relationship.

Event

Though relationships typically progress or regress within the same framework, they can unexpectedly shift, taking a lateral detour and moving along a different tower. It happens because of continuous events happening around us. A person might start as a stranger in the Anchor Tower and progress to becoming a good friend. However, they transform into an adversary due to unforeseen events, following the trajectory towards the Nemesis tower. Shifts often occur in life due to gradual or sudden events that trigger negative feelings and boost a high sense of self-importance in one tower, or conversely, lead to positive emotions and lower ego, guiding the relationship back to the Anchor path. Minor incidents at the tower's base may initiate this transition. Yet, it typically takes a significant event or a succession of events to trigger a horizontal movement between the top of the towers. Hence, it's crucial to remain mindful of the changes in our personal or shared experiences while building a relationship to prevent an unexpected sideways shift in the relationship's direction.

Endnote Reflections

Being an Anchor for someone is a huge responsibility. As a father, I am the anchor for my son, which means I play a unique role in his life. I am the person who's the selfless partner for him, no matter what. I am not just his dad; I am someone he can trust completely and talk to about anything, from small everyday stuff to big, life-changing decisions. My role is to support him. It does not mean I do everything for him or make all his choices. Instead, I am here to help him figure things out independently. When he's facing a tough time or a big challenge, I am the one he can lean on. I listen to him, offer advice when needed, and sometimes remind him that he's not alone.

But being an anchor is not just about helping through the tough times; it's also about celebrating the good ones. When my kid achieves something, whether big, like winning a competition or small, like improving in a subject he struggles with, I cheer him on. It helps him see his value and builds his confidence. My role also involves guiding him as he figures out who he is and what he wants from life. It does not mean I tell him what to do or who to be. Instead, I encourage him to explore his interests, to ask questions, and to think about what kind of person he wants to become. I am here to offer perspectives, but ultimately, his life choices are his own.

Lastly, as his anchor, I am here to provide stability. Life can be unpredictable and sometimes hard to navigate. By being constant in his life, I help him feel secure. This security gives him the foundation to take risks, explore, grow, and eventually find his way in the world and maybe more anchors along the way, offering a different perspective on his purpose in life. Similarly, he has become my anchor.

Notes

Story 14

Seeds In Fruit Of Seed

Through generations, not only does the quality of life's 'tree' improve, but the quality of 'fruit' and seed within it also experiences changes. It mirrors the subtle shifts in the genes across generations. For example, my grandparents supported my father's life as his pillars or anchors. But they weren't the only ones guiding him, as he had several anchors throughout his life. My father passed these experiences and lessons to me, and my mother added her unique perspective. Similarly, Nidhi and I have added our wisdom and insights to what we received from our respective parents and passed them on to our son Ishu. We expect that the originality we have added to our son through these collective lessons will lead to his growth.

If we keep changing how we act and improve others, it's like starting a wave that makes each new generation even better than the last in ways we can't even describe. These incremental adjustments over time can significantly enhance the next generation's capabilities. Just like the Fibonacci sequence, a symbol of progressive growth, interconnectedness, harmony, and improvement, it shows how things grow and connect over time, proving every addition we make forms part of the bigger and better next step.

"Each seed within the fruit carries the legacy of the original seed and more, promising better growth for the next cycle."

Story 15

Dead Now,
Live Later

You might have heard about people who think they'll keep chasing their materialistic dreams today and enjoy these wins later in life. But sometimes, that 'later' never really comes, neither for them nor for their loved ones. I will not list those failed life stories for you – that's not the point. But it will help to ask why this keeps happening to people around us, even though we all know it's wrong. So, unless you understand the root cause, you can not take corrective actions to change the situation, i.e., this means changing what we intake in our DIPOLE cycle.

As you now know, according to the DIPOLE framework, learning is supposed to result from a well-rounded end-to-end process. But when there's a learning imbalance, everything gets thrown off track. It is because learning becomes input to the same iterative process, and incorrect or incomplete learning causes imbalance. The central reason for everyone chasing materialistic dreams is this imbalance in money management learning.

But how does this imbalance in our learning take place? It starts in our childhood. We end up borrowing the wrong knowledge from the people around us. We learn the wrong lessons when we analyse our world against the same faulty rules and knowledge. These lessons drive us towards materialistic gains at an early age because people measure success with financial gains. Hence, we must correct our understanding of money and its management. So what do we do? How do we learn the proper lesson?

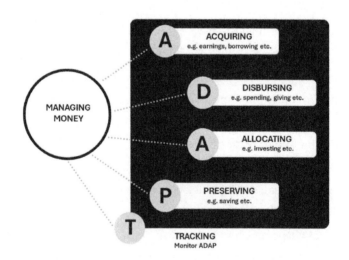

15.1 Managing Money - ADAPT

Acquiring, **D**isbursing, **A**llocating, **P**reserving, **T**racking

ADAPT is one such approach to understanding and managing your money: Acquiring (like earning money or borrowing), Disbursing (which means spending or donating), Allocating (investing money into stocks or savings), Preserving (simply saving it), and Tracking (keeping an eye on what you are doing with your money). Most of us get a mixed bag of lessons from schools or parents. For instance, in many Eastern cultures, people often focus more on acquiring, saving money, and investing. Still, they might skip out on enjoying money or an intelligent way to keep track of it. Meanwhile, in the West, there's much emphasis on spending and investing, and yes, accessing money, often through borrowing. But not so much on saving and tracking. Few learn to balance all parts of money management, i.e. ADAPT.

Acquiring cash seems to be everyone's favourite, both in the East and the West and across the globe. Hence, we are all caught up in making money. This attitude can make us focus too much on one or more activities but not all, leading to a life where we're constantly chasing cash or spending cash. Understanding all five stages of ADAPT is crucial for complete knowledge. It's critical to recognise that besides earning or borrowing money, we must ensure we enjoy life with that income alongside our families. Also, the term ADAPT highlights the need to flexibly change and tailor your financial and life strategies as our economic situation evolves with time, a crucial skill for successful life management.

Therefore, we need to grasp the correct money management principles and educate our children about all five areas of financial stewardship. Doing so will safeguard both our present and future, guaranteeing stability regarding the amount of money we will spend in the future and enjoy better quality of our lives in the present.

> **"Mastering the complexities of money management paves the way for genuine self-care and care of others."**

Endnote Reflections

Some of the strategies I would recommend, based on my experience:

- Start by understanding what a budget is and how to create one. Track all your income (allowance, gifts, job earnings) and expenses (snacks, games, subscriptions). Use apps or a simple notebook to keep track. It helps you see where your money is going and where you might cut back to save more.

- Set specific, achievable goals, like buying a new phone or game or saving for a concert. Decide how much money you need and by when. Then, calculate how much you should save each week or month to reach your goal. It teaches the importance of saving and planning.

- Learn to differentiate between what you need (essentials like food and educational supplies) and what you want (non-essentials like the latest trainers or gadgets). Prioritise spending on your needs before your wants, and think twice before spending money on something that's not essential.

- Find ways to earn money, like part-time jobs, freelancing, or starting a small business, if possible. Earning your own money teaches responsibility and the value of hard work, which gives you a greater appreciation for your cash.
- Teach kids basic investment concepts like stocks, bonds, or savings accounts that earn interest. They do not have to invest real money, but understanding how investments work can prepare them for the future. Some apps and games simulate investing to help them learn without risk.

Notes

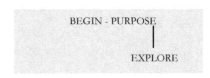
Story 16

Beyond Your Bubble, 'What If' To 'Why Not'

My experience suggests that one should step outside one's comfort zone from time to time to explore life beyond the bubble of usual hangouts and hobbies. There's a whole world beyond what you already know and love. By trying something new, you gain different perspectives and keep your life full of surprises and continuous new learning. With the pace at which the world is changing today, it is more necessary to expose yourself to something new because the things you are into now might not even be around in a few years!

"The key is to encourage exploration outside our usual comfort zone."

The New Kitchen Table

It does not matter if the activity is small; stepping out of our comfort zone offers us a fresh view of events. As discussed in earlier stories, this exploration can benefit those still searching for their passion or purpose.

Take Ishu's story, for example. A few years ago, he played video games and browsed through YouTube. His big dream was to create viral YouTube content. At the same time, I, newly unemployed, was trying to create online courses, a task that pushed me out of my comfort zone. Inspired by my enthusiasm, he started brainstorming ideas with me every night at the kitchen table and started working on his YouTube channel. However, his initial interest waned after a few weeks when he saw only a handful of people were watching his videos and that too only family members. Then, he had a lightbulb moment: if he couldn't go viral himself, why not help others do it and earn some cash? His shift in focus led to his first one-time earnings of $15 from a kid in the US. In this situation, we ended up being $15 rich and making someone else viral by getting 10k views. It taught us a valuable lesson about venturing beyond our comfort zone and picking up new skills, which can open doors to opportunities we never knew existed for us.

This attitude to explore new things led him to try various sports later in life, such as badminton, cricket, football, rugby, and golf. And to add, he was already learning karate and swimming then. Eventually, he found his golf niche and excelled at it. He picked up different training techniques for each sport and made new friends along the way. That gained confidence replicated in his studies as his grades improved. This journey also introduced him to the gym, where he focused on staying fit without bulking up. As a selfless anchor, I supported Ishu in forging his path and exploring everything life offers without being held back by my fears or my wife's. Today, he stands out as the only sports enthusiast in our family for the past ten generations. So, you can see how moving out of his bubble opened up new growth opportunities for him.

One evening, when we sat at the kitchen table chatting about exploring something new, the discussion about fulfilling my long-standing dream of authoring a book resurfaced. Though I hesitated with doubts and several 'what ifs', I tentatively floated the idea to the family. It required a committed focus on writing, potentially necessitating a break from my paid employment. The risks were high, and the financial outcomes were uncertain, though the chance of personal and family growth was high. At that time, Ishu's classic one-liner response made the difference. He said, "Dad, why not? I will work with you." Thus, 'The New Kitchen Table' was born.

Endnote Reflections

- Always encourage yourself to make a change. This change should be something that is out of your comfort zone.

- Find a buddy to join you on this new adventure for extra motivation. They could be someone who knows the ropes, has been through the changes you're aiming for, or even someone new to it all, there to be your cheerleader. This way, you all get to learn something new together.

- Venture out and socialise. Initiate long conversations with individuals around you. You need to take advantage of the chance to meet interesting individuals.

- Another example is that you sometimes stick to different restaurants. Explore various spots and taste different cuisines. While eating, ponder how the chef prepared the dish and whether you could recreate it or make it even better at home. This method has taught me to cook many meals myself. My motto? 'If I can taste it, I can make it.'

- Do not stress over the possibility of failing again, even if you have stumbled ten times before or if a million others have yet to succeed in the same effort. It's essential to take a shot and embrace calculated risks. Another failure in a sea of many won't shift the balance, but becoming that one success story can make a difference.

Story 17

Life Flight,
Only Limited Baggage Please

Through perspective, we observe our surroundings. It shapes our interpretation and response to various life events. I aim to share an anecdote with you, which I used to explain on one occasion to Ishu, to illustrate how altering perspective can forever transform your life's growth.

In my over twenty years of experience in professional environments, I've learnt that competition is fierce— sometimes brutally so. But one of the biggest lessons I've learnt is the harm holding onto your grudges can do. It's like carrying an invisible weight on your shoulders, slowing you down and stopping you from achieving your full potential. These negative feelings consume your thoughts and energy, leaving less room for positive actions and growth.

"Often, our problems are not problems at all but reflections of our misunderstandings."

I once conflicted with a colleague. It was not personal but the principles of running projects at work. He believed in his focus on individual recognition, and I believed in team recognition, which I thought was best for everyone. This disagreement escalated to the point where we stopped talking, which was never a good idea in such scenarios, despite being on the same team and sitting beside each other. This battle did not just affect us; it dampened the entire team's morale, especially since we were both senior technical members with significant influence on the project.

Then, something happened that ultimately changed my perspective about holding grudges. My colleague was in an accident and ended up in the hospital. Not having him in the office that day made me feel happy, and initially, my reaction was one of satisfaction; looking back, I am not proud of my thoughts. I forgot that I was setting the wrong example for my team members and going against my principles of team spirit. But then, I had a minor accident myself, which led to a moment of self-reflection. I realised how petty and harmful my grudges were—to him and myself. I finally decided to visit my colleague in the hospital, putting aside all the negative feelings. That decision did not just help mend our relationship; it lifted a weight on my shoulders that I did not even realise I was carrying. From that moment, I promised myself to change my perspective and not to hold on to grudges, as they serve no purpose other than to hold me back from my progress and affect the happiness of others, too. As I highlighted in the NEAT Relationships framework, events or series of events can convert your worst enemy into a friend and beyond. This act of mine led to both of us becoming good friends.

The moral here? Changing your perspective—how you view a situation—can impact your life in multiple ways. Shifting your outlook improves your well-being and opens new pathways to success. Remember that life is too short to live with unwanted dead-end conflicts. Shifting your viewpoint doesn't mean overlooking what's real; it involves opting for a new lens to see through beyond immediate frustrations. This mindset shift will lead you faster towards peace and a more fulfilling, relaxing, and complete life.

Endnote Reflections

- Recognise that every person you encounter has a role in your life, even if it's unclear in the present moment. They might be there to teach you a lesson and to help you grow.

- Adopting new habits becomes more manageable if you change your perspective. It's normal for change to feel awkward or difficult. Keep at it; with time, this new way of thinking will become a natural part of you.

- Always function as if someone younger is watching your actions. Think about the lessons your actions will teach them. Ensure you're setting a good example and that your actions reflect the qualities you want to pass on to them.

- If something you're doing is causing you anxiety and keeping you up at night, it's probably not beneficial for you in the long run. Actions leading to unwanted stress and unnecessary discomfort will likely harm you and need immediate attention.
- Aim to maintain an open mindset to pass on a legacy of positivity rather than stress and negativity.

Story 18

Home In Flow,
When All In Element

A house becomes a home when everyone is in the happy and uplifting zone; without that, let us say, it's just a well-furnished office with too many snack breaks between war games. There are some places where you feel at ease as soon as you walk in; you can imagine spending your whole life there, just chilling. But then, there are other places where you feel uneasy even before stepping inside, wondering why you did not just skip the visit altogether. Ever wonder why that is?

Let's try a quick thought experiment. Picture your imaginary family of four. Today was a fantastic day for everyone. You're over the moon because you just got a promotion, a big raise, and lots of praise at work. It's your best day ever professionally. Your partner had a similar win at their job. Your kids aced their tests, won a sports trophy, and made an awesome new friend. Everyone comes home excited, like you're all walking on air, and the future looks incredibly bright. It feels like everything in life is just clicking simultaneously, pushing all of you towards something better. Now, you're all gathering around the kitchen table. Imagine how everyone's feeling. What's the overall vibe at home? Unique and beautiful.

Moreover, you decide to listen instead of jumping to share your news. You let your partner and kids go first, soaking in their happiness, saving your story for last because you want them to enjoy their moment. That right there? That's the warmth and joy of a home when everyone's in their happy place, filled with genuine love for each other. You can spend your entire life with this family.

Now, let us flip the script. It's the same extraordinary day, but this time, everyone's trying to outdo each other with their stories. It's a competition of who had the best day, with everyone talking over each other, each person trying to grab the spotlight. Imagine the atmosphere now around the kitchen table. Everyone's technically in their zone, but instead of lifting each other, it feels like someone has sucked the energy out of the room. The table is not happy anymore; it feels more like a tense, competitive workplace. So, what vibe are you all generating now? Do you want to stay with this family?

Did you notice the difference in your feeling now? The first scenario is what home should feel like, and the second is something else entirely. Call that home your office if you want.

Home In Flow, When All In Element

Let us use the same scenario for your body. Imagine your body as a team, each organ doing its job. When everything's working together smoothly, without any part trying to hog the spotlight, you feel fantastic – healthy and happy. You generate a positive aura around you. Anyone coming into your area of influence can experience that vibe. But what if one part starts throwing a fit? Your heart, "I've been pumping non-stop for years, but does anyone notice? No. What if I stop?" Or imagine your brain getting all high and feeling superior, saying, "I am the boss here. I do all the thinking and directing. If I stop, everything stops." Or think about your stomach complaining about always having to break down food. I never get any thanks from anyone and get blamed for bad dumps every morning. What would happen if these parts stopped working, one by one, just because they felt unappreciated? There would be chaos in your body, right? Every part of your body, just like every person in a family, is significant and needs to work together without any single one acting as if they are the only one that matters.

Now, let's break it down with some simple math equations.

- When everyone is happy and positive

Home1 Energy = (Dad Energy + Mom Energy + Child1 Energy + Child2 Energy) + Other unknown factors

- When one person is negative

Home2 Energy = (Dad Energy - Mom Energy + Child1 Energy + Child2 Energy) + Other unknown factors

The New Kitchen Table

There are no marks for guessing that Home1 > Home2, keeping everything else constant.

It shows how one negative vibe can bring down the entire home's energy. Before you know it, everyone starts catching the negativity bug—arguing, silent tension, sad faces, and even health problems start creeping in. And what happens when these gloomy folks step outside? They end up spreading that gloom, pulling others down, too, and soon, everyone around you and your family starts feeling down. What will the overall learning and growth be when this situation goes into the DIPOLE cycle?

Have you ever noticed how when one person litters on the street, it suddenly becomes a free-for-all dumping ground? One empty bag leads to more rubbish, and suddenly, that spot's a mess because everyone thinks it's okay to add to the pile. That's what happens with a downbeat home—it does not just affect you; it also attracts negativity from the outside, turning your space into a dumping ground for bad vibes. Can you avoid twisting your life into a cluttered street corner?

Everyone has a unique role, contributing to the home's overall vibe. Everyone in a home has a task that keeps the home's energy welcoming and uplifting. The same is true with our bodies; if our bodies are in harmony, we become welcoming and uplifting to the people around us. People would love to stay around you; some may decide to live with you forever.

Endnote Reflections

- Always keep your self-talk and comments to others positive. It's ok to offer criticism, but make sure it's helpful and constructive, aiming to solve problems and share knowledge rather than tear someone down. If you can't reduce suffering in the lives of others, do not become the reason for creating a dumping ground.

- Avoid passing your bad moods or negative thoughts on others. Spreading a lousy mood leads to a toxic environment, like a growing pile of rubbish nobody wants to be around.

- Only some people need your intervention to fix their problems. Just like a monkey might not understand the use of a dog's tail, it does not mean that the dog's tail is a problem, and it gives the monkey the right to make fun of it.

- Focus on improving the lives of your family and others. When you step outside, aim to bring back only what will make your household happier. You wipe your feet on a doormat to keep your home clean. Next time when you wipe your feet, wipe your mind with it before entering your beautiful home.

Notes

Story 19

Tears Of Night,
Broken By Sunrise

Right before exams, I was a train wreck, constantly crying and convinced I'd fail. Ishu, though, is different. It's not that he never worries – he does – but mostly, he's confident, believing in his prep and aiming for the best grades possible. Whenever I was a mess as a child, crying over my exams, my dad had his unique way of dealing with me. He'd say, "Amit, if crying is going to help, let all of us collectively have a good cry together, and maybe that'll magically get you the grades you want." And when I was freaking out because dinner was late at the kitchen table, acting like I'd starve to death, he'd throw out, "Why not play some hunger games?" – and nope, this was way before any Hunger Games movies or books; we're talking over 40 years ago. But now, 40 years later, I understand his message and realise how deep they were. I figured my dad was pushing the motto 'work hard, do not cry' and 'cook something for yourself and others.'

So, no matter how clever or prepared we are, life sometimes creates chaos. We will face hurt, be tested, and probably feel down or blame ourselves when things go south. It's like going through autumn, losing all our leaves, and feeling bare and numb. And sometimes, no matter what we try or who we turn to for help – coaches, psychologists, friends – it feels like nothing can pull us out of that dark place. Do not cry, but find ways to resolve the situation.

I've been stuck in this rut a few times, endlessly trying to refresh my circumstances but feeling like the night drags on. I've experimented with various strategies to escape these tough spots. Honestly, I did not just come up with these methods on my own. Looking back, I am unsure how I learnt about them – maybe from conversations, films, or elsewhere. But I've taken the time to dig into their origins.

"Allow time to renew; with each passing day, peace will return to you."

It would be best if you had time to rejuvenate after complex events. Take the necessary time and do not rush the process. Healing takes time, but it will happen. You cannot afford to confront chaos with a malfunctioning DIPOLE cycle, but if you find yourself amid chaos, ensure that you emerge with refined thoughts. The universe has allowed you to reflect and eliminate what no longer serves you. Let go of unnecessary emotions, thoughts, and relationships.

Endnote Reflections

Depending on your life and health condition, you can try out one or more of these strategies. Some might need you to seek professional guidance or do your research, but they're all worth exploring. It's interesting to note that many of these techniques have roots in regions that have faced incredibly harsh challenges, whether due to human actions or natural disasters. And who better to learn resilience from than those who have survived such ordeals?

- **Shinrin-yoku (Forest Bathing)**—This Japanese practice focuses on getting closer to one's natural environment. It involves going into nature and taking the time to relax and breathe deeply. The concept suggests that time with nature can alleviate stress and improve mental strength.

- **Yoga and Pranayama**—Yoga is an ancient Indian practice that combines physical postures, meditation, and breathing techniques called Pranayama. It's all about creating balance in the body and mind, improving focus, and reducing stress. Give your mind a break while stretching and strengthening your body.

- **Qi Gong**—Qi Gong is a Chinese wellness practice that combines movement, meditation, and regulated breathing to enhance energy flow in the body. It is also known as Qi. It is a moving meditation that helps you relax and feel more energised at the same time.

- **Banya (Russian Sauna)**—Banya is a traditional Russian sauna experience. It involves sitting in a hot, steamy room, followed by a cool plunge. It may remind you of your gym with a sauna and pool. It's a social activity that relaxes the muscles and clears the mind.

- **Capoeira**—If you like music and acrobatics with elements of dance, then try Capoeira, a Brazilian martial art. It's not just fighting; it's more about moving your body in a flow, learning how to flow with others, and expressing yourself.

- **Ubuntu Philosophy**—Ubuntu is a South African term meaning "I am because we are." It's a philosophy focusing on community, connection, and mutual caring for all. By embracing Ubuntu, you recognise the importance of relationships, kindness, and empathy in community well-being.

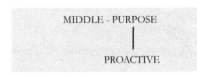

Story 20

Defining Chaos, Identify Wired Patterns

Identifying patterns within chaos can significantly improve your life by enhancing your ability to predict, prepare for, and manage complex situations more effectively. I have identified four essential areas to identify patterns in a set of random events. Acknowledging the influence of 'Culture,' engaging in deep 'Reflection,' recognising events 'Interconnectedness,' and identifying early 'Signals,' help me navigate the uncertainty of chaos. These elements help me foresee potential challenges and respond proactively. Focusing on these factors not only prepares me for immediate issues but also enhances my ability to handle future uncertainties, transforming chaos into a navigable and understandable path.

Rather than immediately responding to chaos, the priority should be to identify patterns within it.

- ## Culture

Culture is fundamentally composed of the shared habits, traditions, and norms that shape both your identity and that of others involved in chaos. It consists of a broad spectrum of elements, from the languages you speak to the implicit rules instilled through your upbringing. Naturally, culture influences how you perceive and navigate situations. Digging deep into your understanding of your cultural background, as well as that of others, is crucial for recognizing patterns and crafting the proper responses to chaotic situations. This comprehensive grasp of cultural dynamics allows for a better interpretation of events and enhances your ability to manage and adapt to the complexities of diverse environments.

- ## Reflection

Focusing on the events around you and posing meaningful, open-ended questions can deepen your understanding of chaotic situations. By carefully analysing your responses to these questions, you draw nearer to the core of the chaos, prompting a comprehensive examination. This approach leads you closer to grasping the 'Why?' behind the chaos. Consider the example of losing a job; although it appears as a single event, it often triggers a cascade of challenges, including mental stress, financial strain, and societal pressure. Reflecting on questions like, "Why was I let go? When did the indicators first appear? Were there any warnings?" is crucial. While your immediate focus may be on dealing with the chaos of job loss, reviewing past events to pinpoint where things began to unravel can better prepare you for the future. This reflection helps you identify trends and recognize patterns in the events leading up to your job loss. You might have overlooked these patterns initially, but a collective review after the event can reveal patterns clearly. Remember, even slight adjustments in how you frame these questions can significantly influence your reactions to these events and their interpreted meanings.

• **Interconnectedness**

As you may have noticed from my personal stories, a series of events initially may feel chaotic; however, with close observation, you can find connections. Events in our lives are all connected through a series of visible and invisible links. By recognising these links, you can trace the ripple effects of your actions and see how they influence you. Identifying these connections can guide you towards the appropriate solutions and resources needed to resolve the issue at hand. This awareness not only aids in navigating your immediate chaos but also enhances your ability to respond wisely to future events of a similar nature.

• **Signal**

Signals or clues guide your brain to interpret events through the lens of past experiences, functioning like smoke alarms to prevent significant disasters by alerting you before everything escalates. A seemingly random event might later emerge as a crucial element of a larger pattern. Therefore, it is vital to monitor and connect these events closely. For example, if certain situations at work consistently lead to stress, early recognition of these signals can prompt a timely and effective response. These signals serve as signposts, directing your actions. When you notice similar events beginning to unfold, they provide a clear indication to intervene and perhaps steer in a new direction. It's like observing the sky before leaving the house and taking an umbrella due to the potential for rain. Suppose the rain occurs, improving your knowledge of forecasting. Similarly, by continuously testing your signals, you can reach a point where, much like weather forecasting, you can better anticipate future events.

Endnote Reflections

One key outcome from the identified patterns of chaotic events is the agility to adjust. You become better at adapting to fast-changing situations when things strike you unplanned. Adapting to changing events ensures that your fast actions remain relevant and practical. I have regularly used these factors to identify patterns within the chaos of my life. Continually analysing these factors has helped me to find recurring themes and connections which we sometimes overlook. This ongoing observation and particular behavioural action allows for gradually unveiling patterns amid randomness. It helps me to understand complex situations better and craft solutions more in tune with the event's complexities, turning seemingly isolated incidents into parts of a larger, understandable pattern.

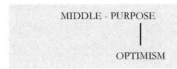
Story 21

Path To Finding Optimism

My family and I have tried to maintain an optimistic outlook on life consistently. My friends always find us confident and have encouraged me to share my thoughts by writing a chapter on Optimism in this book. Here is the secret of our optimism and proactiveness – the **'Optimism Matrix.'** The 'Optimism Matrix' is to help you proactively assess and learn about your life choices and actions through the intersection of four critical dimensions: Health, Money, Purpose, and Time. This matrix serves as a guide to understanding how access to various resources and maintaining focus on crucial life aspects can contribute to a more optimistic lifestyle. Health and Money form the foundational axis in this framework, suggesting that well-being and financial stability are essential for care, security and opportunity. The horizontal axis emphasises the importance of keeping sight of Time and Purpose, indicating that awareness of our finite time and clear personal goals are crucial for sharing wisdom, guiding strength and inspiring influence. These elements create a comprehensive approach to realising a positive outgrowth. By giving care, guiding strength, creating opportunities, and inspiring influence, the Optimism Matrix outlines a balanced strategy for being proactive in making life choices.

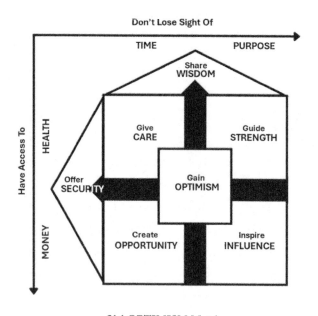

21.1 OPTIMISM Matrix

When you align the elements from the Optimism Matrix — Health, Money, Purpose, and Time — and ensure you are aware of them while not losing sight of the importance of these core elements, you create positivity in your life and the ability to bring change to the lives of people around you. But what is Optimism, and why do we need to be optimistic? Optimism is not just a feel-good emotion; it's the crucial strategic resource in your life that grows with a balance of the four elements which will drive meaningful growth. When you have access to health, you have the well-being necessary to engage with the world meaningfully. Access to money provides stability and the means to explore opportunities and extend generosity to others. Access to purpose gives a sense of direction, infusing your actions with meaning and inspiring those around you. Recognising the value of time ensures that you prioritise what is important to you, leading to more satisfying and impactful results.

Each of these elements contributes to optimism by improving individual circumstances and creating an environment around you where you can thrive and facilitate the well-being of everyone. When people are optimistic, they're more likely to approach life events with a solution-oriented mindset and see opportunities in adverse conditions. This perspective is infectious; it can motivate and elevate those in your vicinity, generating a wave of positive transformation within your network and beyond.

Matrix also guides you when you have an imbalance, i.e., you are strong in one aspect compared to others, and it shows how combining these aspects can help you decide which action in your life will bring balance and meaning.

Security (Health + Money) - This quadrant implies that when people have access to both good health and financial resources, they experience a sense of security.

Good health provides the physical and mental foundation to enjoy life and engage in activities while having sufficient money, which offers stability, contributing to overall security. If you are in this quadrant, you are generally happy with life but lack time and purpose. You may be more inward-focused, leading to a sense of emptiness and always searching for that meaning. The solution for you is to spend a portion of your health and money for the security of others, i.e., a little outward-focused. This act of yours will give you a chance to discover your purpose in life.

"Balance of Health, Money, Purpose, and Time brings Optimism."

Care (Health + Time) - This part of the matrix suggests that having both time and good health enables you to offer care. Extra time allows you to focus on health, practice self-care, and extend support and care to loved ones, enhancing societal well-being. Your presence in this quadrant suggests that you are more outward-focused. You care for others because you have the suitable condition to do it, which may become your full-time job, but it does not pay you enough to do things you mean to do. You want to enjoy life, travel, build your own house, have a nice car, and feel materialistic happiness like everyone else. It would help if you had money and purpose to bring complete optimism. You can join hands with those who have access to funds and share the same sense of purpose as you do. It will give you a sense of security, bring strength and opportunities for you, and increase your area of influence.

Wisdom (Time + Purpose) - Having more time and a sense of purpose means you are better than most because you have achieved a state that many envy. You have discovered the art of time management and are wise enough to know what you want to do in this life. It is something that all of us would like to learn from you, and if you can find a formula to share with everyone around you, you can get more access to money.

Influence (Purpose + Money) - This quadrant indicates that you have financial resources aligned with a clear sense of purpose, and you can influence and guide others to join you in the more significant cause. You can create a more considerable impact in the world around you, for example, by providing financial means to the young generation with better access to time and health. If you think you are in this quadrant, you could be the world's thought leader, unite everyone to a common cause, and then fund that cause or mission to bring positive change. You can ignite the fire in others by joining the mission and, in the process, help them find their purpose.

Opportunity (Money + Time) - The intersection of financial stability and time availability can help you create opportunities. You have the right fuel to supply to those who are clear in their purpose but do not have money to support their cause. Like folks in Dragon's Den, you can create the right growth engine to fund innovations and use your area of influence and power to bring security to a larger society.

Strength (Purpose + Health) - This suggests that when people are healthy and have a clear sense of purpose, their moral compass can strengthen others to bring the impact that the world needs. With this, you can create whatever you want in this life. If you want to be a monk living in a monastery, you will be the best; if you want to be the next business tycoon, you will be one. Good health provides the energy and vitality to pursue your purpose. In contrast, a strong sense of purpose guides actions and decisions, allowing you to lead by example and inspire strength in others.

Collectively, these elements illustrate that having balanced access to time, money, health, and purpose leads to an overall sense of **OPTIMISM**. Each factor contributes uniquely to well-being, and when harmonised, it enhances one's ability to remain hopeful, proactive, and optimistic about the future.

The 'Optimism Matrix' also incorporates two crucial guiding principles along its axes: the vertical axis, 'Have Access To,' and the horizontal axis, 'Do Not Lose Sight Of.'

The vertical axis **'Have Access To'** represents the resources and elements vital for an individual's well-being and potential to generate optimism: Money and Health. The key idea here is not merely possessing these resources but, more importantly, having access to them. It involves utilising or leveraging these aspects effectively in your life. The concept extends beyond having money in your bank, most notably having access to financial resources or knowing the opportunities for economic stability. It could include support systems, community resources, credit, investments, or education that can lead to earning potential. It also means having the opportunity to borrow money for growth and not just for consumption. Access to good health means being free from illness and accessing healthcare, nutritious food, clean water, and environments or habits that promote physical and mental well-being.

The horizontal axis **'Do Not Lose Sight Of'** principle emphasises the importance of focusing on life's critical elements: Time and Purpose. It's a reminder to avoid getting so caught up in the day-to-day small material gains. It's crucial to understand the value of time, to use it wisely, and to ensure that how you spend your time aligns with your priorities and goals. Time is a non-renewable resource, and learning to utilise it wisely can pave the way for a more efficient lifestyle. Purpose reminds you to reflect on and stay true to your path continually. Even when faced with challenges or commencing various life paths, you should remember the underlying reasons or motivations driving your actions and decisions.

Endnote Reflections

Gaining Optimism is seen as a holistic concept influenced by various external and internal factors. Maintaining access to necessary resources while not losing sight of all four elements allows us to lead balanced, forward-moving, and hopeful lives. The Optimism Matrix guides you to a balanced and reflective approach to life where access to essential resources (like health and money) is as significant as the conscious use and appreciation of time and adherence to your life purpose (meaningful pursuits). We can navigate life more optimistically by ensuring access to these fundamental needs, consistently reflecting on our time and purpose, and making decisions that lead to growth, satisfaction, and overall well-being.

Story 22

Empty Vessel Is Filled, You Just Can't See

Often, we might look at someone and think they have nothing to offer, labelling them as an 'empty vessel.' However, our perception of the person can be misleading, and it's usually due to something I refer to as the **'Blind Brain' phenomenon**. A 'Blind Brain' clouds our vision and thoughts. It is wearing tinted glasses that only show us what we want to see. Because of 'Blind Brain', we overlook the unique qualities and contributions of the person in question.

Have you ever overlooked someone because they seemed too different and later discovered that they were incredible? It is due to your 'Blind Brain' in action. It prevents you from recognising others' good qualities, not because these people lack outstanding characteristics, but because we've never encountered something like that before, becoming trapped in our own experiences, assumptions, and stereotypes.

Everyone has something unique to offer. Differences do not make someone less valuable; they add to the richness and diversity of our experiences. By challenging our views and opening our minds to diverse views, we can begin to appreciate everyone's worth. This perspective shift can change how we interact with people around us. So, the next time you think of someone as an 'empty vessel,' remember they have unique insights and qualities. Changing our viewpoint can make us look at empty vessels as sources of wisdom and inspiration, enriching our learning and reducing the size of our 'Blind Brain.'

In meetings, I usually remain quiet if the discussion is straightforward and does not require my specific insights, especially when everyone else seems to have something to say. Also, I do not buy into tactics like taking all the credit for others' work or blaming someone else when things go wrong. Because of my stance, fitting in with the rest of the corporate culture can sometimes become challenging. This difference in approach can lead to being seen as a hindrance in the eyes of others, who may perceive me as lacking corporate leadership qualities or an empty vessel. But when everything is falling apart, deadlines are not met, team members are leaving, and there seems to be no clear solution to endless problems, people look towards me to bail them out. That is when this empty vessel suddenly looks filled to everyone and becomes a lifesaver.

Empty Vessel Is Filled, You Just Can't See

We often dismiss someone as irrelevant in specific scenarios simply because we have not tried to understand them. But, as you take the time to connect, you might discover that these individuals have rare skills and traits that 99% of people do not – they do not fit into the usual categories of ordinary people because they are extraordinary. It is widespread for truly gifted individuals to undergo such responses from people around them. They stand out because they do not slot neatly into the conventional outlook that society expects. The issue is not with these exceptional minds; it is with those of us who fail to recognise their value because their brilliance does not present in a way that immediately grabs our attention and makes sense to us.

"When you label someone an empty vessel, think your 'Blind Brain' is in action."

Endnote Reflections

- Exceptional individuals often share unique perspectives or solutions. Active listening helps you catch subtle hints of their unconventional thinking or unique skills.

- Those with unique abilities might approach situations differently, demonstrating creativity or efficiency that sets them apart.

- Ask questions to encourage detailed responses, not just 'yes' or 'no.' This can reveal a person's thought process, creativity, and depth of knowledge.

- Those with exceptional skills often shine when you assign challenging tasks that require innovative solutions.
- Encourage individuals to reveal their unique skills without fear of judgment from you. These individuals with exceptional skills are often passionate about specific areas or subjects.

Story 23

Living With The Tiger

Power of The Tiger

Once, in a jungle, a man found himself lost and terrified. He looked up to the heavens with trembling hands and prayed for divine intervention. "God," he pleaded, "help me please! I am your honest and faithful child. Save me." God responded, "I will grant you one wish, but here is my warning. Once I fulfil your wish, I cannot take it back; you cannot harm it and must work with it forever or face the consequences." The man, desperate for companionship and power to deal with his fear, hastily wished for a loyal companion who would make him appear mighty so he could enjoy his stay in the jungle. Without delay, a tiger walked before him with its mesmerising golden eyes.

"Master," the tiger spoke, bowing its head, "tell me, what can I do for you?" With the tiger by his side, the man started executing his plans to rule the jungle. His newfound companion instilled fear in the hearts of all creatures, and soon, the man became the most powerful being. The man aged and became weaker as the years passed, but the

tiger grew stronger. The man's dependency on the tiger grew due to his diminishing health. Sleep became a luxury he dared not indulge in for fear of the tiger turning on him and the other jungle inhabitants seeking revenge. Due to desperation and old age, the man pleaded with God to get rid of the tiger and grant him the friendship of the other jungle creatures instead.

One fateful night, as exhaustion finally overcame him, the man slept. The tiger seized its opportunity. And so, the man who sought power and companionship met his demise at the hands of the very creature he had summoned for his benefit.

Here, the man represents us, and the tiger symbolises power.

I emphasise that four essential areas demand our attention and readiness in the quest to enjoy power. Neglecting any while focusing solely on another could lead us to the same destiny as the man in the above story.

"Design a system that operates with a key, not a kick."

1. Reason for Wanting Power

Why do you desire power? Understanding your motives is critical in shaping how you exercise your power. See if you recognise the points below as your reason for wanting power.

- You are seeking power for the validation of accomplishments and the acknowledgement of success.
- You desire power to exert influence, establish authority, enjoy, and ensure stability.
- You aspire to use power as a force for positive change,

leaving a lasting legacy and achieving immortality through your actions.

- Pursuing power to validate your worth, boost self-esteem, and assert dominance in competitive environments.
- Seeking power to overcome vulnerability, escape difficult circumstances, and take control of your destiny.

2. Means of Acquiring Power

How will you attain power? It involves the methods and actions you take to achieve it.

- Through education, training, and personal development initiatives, you acquire knowledge, expertise, and practical skills. This empowers you to excel in your chosen fields and gain recognition for competence and proficiency.
- You build solid connections and establish positive relationships with influential individuals, mentors, and peers. Networking allows you to leverage social capital, access opportunities, and expand your sphere of influence, increasing your power and impact.
- Developing leadership qualities for the ability to inspire, motivate, and mobilise others towards common goals. Influential leaders can exert influence, navigate complex situations, and drive change within organisations and communities, thus enhancing their power and authority.
- You demonstrate sound judgment, foresight, and the ability to manage risks effectively. You are also perceived as a competent and trustworthy leader, increasing your power and credibility.

3. Living with Power

What will life be like once you have power? It is crucial to consider the responsibilities and consequences that come with it.

- With power comes the ability to influence and impact the world around you. Your decisions and actions can shape your thoughts, drive change, and affect the lives of others in positive or negative ways.

- Having power gives a significant responsibility. You will be accountable for your decisions and their consequences, and you must consider the welfare of others as you impart your authority.

- As a person in power, others will closely scrutinise your actions. Maintaining transparency, integrity, and accountability in all your dealings is essential to uphold trust and credibility.

- Life with power can be challenging and complex. You will face difficult decisions, navigate competing interests, and encounter resistance or criticism. It's crucial to approach these challenges with resilience, adaptability, and a commitment to ethical leadership.

4. Maintaining Your Power

How will you sustain your power? Power requires upkeep and management to remain relevant.

- Stay current with new trends, advancements, and industry standards. Constantly enhance your abilities, understanding, and tactics to stay pertinent and efficient in evolving circumstances.

- Cultivate solid and positive relationships with key stakeholders, allies, and supporters. Maintain open lines of communication, collaborate on common goals, and seek feedback to strengthen your connections and influence.

- Show integrity in all your actions and decisions. Act with transparency, fairness, and honesty to earn trust and credibility, which is essential for sustaining power over the long term.

- To maintain a competitive edge and drive growth, encourage experimentation, embrace new ideas, and adapt to emerging challenges and opportunities.

- Develop robust strategic plans and risk management strategies to foresee and reduce potential risks to your power and influence. Stay proactive in identifying risks, seizing opportunities, and navigating uncertainties to remain in power.

Endnote Reflections

While many resources can teach you about grabbing power (the second point), few will explore why you seek power, how to navigate life with it, and how to sustain it. These aspects are equally important but often overlooked. Recognising that wishes to gain control can be fulfilled in various ways, sometimes unexpectedly, but before making a wish, prepare yourself to live with it.

Notes

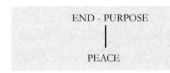

Story 24

Brain, Gut, & X
Keeps Me Alive

Out of the blue, one day, at the Kitchen table, Ishu brought up the time when he could not talk. I am sure you recall the story. He asked me many questions: "Dad, what happened after I started talking? How did I begin putting sentences together? How did I start communicating with you? What was the first thing I ever learnt from you to say?" Before I dive into these fascinating questions, let me share a story with you.

<u>Grandpa's Box</u>

A boy saw a special locked box containing secret treasures with Grandpa. The boy always thought about the box and wished to open it to see everything inside. But he hesitated to ask his grandpa for the key. He felt that Grandpa might give him the box and key one day.

As time went by, the boy grew, but the box stayed closed. One day, his grandpa got extremely sick and did not have much time left with him. The boy knew he had to show courage to ask, or he might never see what was inside the box.

He courageously went to his grandpa and said, "Grandpa, I want to see what's inside the box. Please give me the key so that I can open the box."

With a warm smile, Grandpa said, "My dear boy, this lock does not need a key."

The boy was puzzled. "But, Grandpa, it's locked," he said.

Grandpa replied, "Pull the lock to open the box."

So, the boy pulled the lock, and, to his surprise, it opened! The lock was just a lever to open the box — it was never really locked.

The boy was amazed but also a bit upset. "Grandpa, why did you not tell me?"

Grandpa laughed and said, "Son, you never expressed 'I want.'"

And that is when the boy learnt something particularly significant — sometimes, all you must do is ask for what you want.

So, now that you know the origin of his first sentence let's go back to Ishu's question. I started him off with the sentence 'I want.' It was simple for him to say, giving him a way to communicate with us and showing us his thoughts and needs. It also taught him an important lesson: if he desires something, all he must do is express it, either to himself or to others, by saying, 'I want.'

We have countless boxes in our minds, easily opened with the words "I want." But we have placed imaginary locks on each of these boxes. You might wonder, "How do we know if these boxes exist in our brains?" Human brains are fundamentally the same, tracing back to a common origin billions of years ago. Despite humanity's diverse paths, we share this universal starting point. So, when an individual uncovers something from the universe, the same is accessible to all because we are interconnected with one universe.

A billionaire can tap into the same mental resources you have; the distinction is their decision to declare, 'I want this,' and open their selected box. This knowledge is accessible to everyone. Now, you might try to follow in the footsteps of successful people, adopting their habits or learning from their lives. You will be surprised to know that it is already with you. The essential step is to declare 'I want' to yourself and allow the universe to guide you in opening the box. Discover this truth before it is too late.

Notes

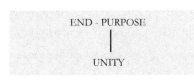

Story 25

I Survived In Thoughts, What Else Do I Need?

You heard me say in the previous story that if you ask your universe, it will grant what you seek. But then you may question it, "I ask to be a millionaire all the time, yet here I am, still not one. And problems in my life? They keep piling up." It feels like you are in a never-ending game. I have shared personal stories before, and I will share more to prove that you have everything it takes to achieve what you want in life.

Let me break this down with another example to get my point across. If I ask you, "When were you born?" most of you would probably tell me your birthday. A few might mention the day they were conceived. But if you ask me, you started even before that. You were in the cards long before your parents met, even before they were born, back when your ancestors dreamt of future generations.

That is right. Your existence was pencilled into the

149

universe's grand plan when your great-great-grandparents decided they would have kids and who would then have their kids. Back then, you did not have a body, clothes, luxury items, or friends—you had nothing and were just a thought. Yet, here you are, a result of wishes and dreams passed down through generations.

So, when I say you have always meant to be here, your arrival was set into motion generations ago, not just on your birth date. You started as an idea, a hope in the universe, and you came into existence without needing anything material. It shows that long before you had anything physical, you were already part of a grand plan—proving that the universe does respond, even if it is in ways we do not immediately see.

Just like that, what you are thinking and wishing for today might not show up next year or even in a hundred years, but eventually, it will come to life because you have set the groundwork. You have opened that box, and once it's open, it stays open for all future generations to make it happen. Someone in your universe will someday bring your thoughts and dreams into reality.

> **"You stand on the
> hopes of your ancestors;
> let your dreams be the hope
> for future generations."**

You might say, "But I won't be around to see it happen."

I Survived In Thoughts, What Else Do I Need?

That's true; you might not be there to see it in person. But your ideas and dreams have a life beyond your own. Just like you are the result of your ancestors' hopes and decisions, your dreams could shape the future for others to come. Planting seeds for a garden you might never see but will grow and benefit future generations. Your impact extends beyond your time here; it centres around contributing to a larger story.

Gifted life from a broken pot

Many generations ago, a clay pot was in a quiet hilltop village. It was no ordinary pot; it was a mystery to all, for no one knew where it came from. The pot did not know what its purpose was. One day, the pot began to roll down the hill. Stones hit it, laughed at by the plants and trees, and even kicked around by the animals. Despite this, it kept rolling, undeterred.

As it reached the bottom of the hill, the inevitable happened – the pot shattered into countless pieces. Lying broken, it wept, not understanding its purpose or why its journey had ended in such a way. Nevertheless, nature had assigned a purpose to the broken pot.

During a fierce thunderstorm, the broken pieces of the pot filled with rainwater and sand. Miraculously, these pieces began to serve its purpose. Birds that once mocked it now drank water from it. The fragments became a nurturing ground for beautiful plants, offering a home to seeds and small creatures. The pot found a new life in its brokenness, becoming a source of life and beauty for the beings that once ridiculed it.

Notes

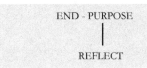

END - PURPOSE

REFLECT

Story 26

Unseen Connections,
Shape Our Lives

Reflect on those moments when you either stumbled upon a random act of kindness or were the architect of one yourself. These minor acts, seemingly trivial at the time, can be invisible threads connecting hearts, leaving a lasting mark on both the benefactor and beneficiary. They reshape our perspectives, beliefs, and actions in subtle yet significant ways in life to come.

Let me take you back to my college days when I had 50 rupees of pocket money in my pocket and felt like I was rich. To give you a sense of inflation, back then, a cup of tea cost me a mere rupee at the local college tea stall— in the present day, you would be forking out 100 rupees for the same pleasure! It was during my second year of college, marked by my strong budgeting skills. After covering my basic expenses, I would save 10 rupees for a movie with pals by month's end. While my friends, flaunting their royal allowances of 200 rupees, could afford three movies a month, I was the group's financial underdog.

On one occasion, which shaped how I live my life today, I found myself 20 miles from home after a movie outing. It was 6 p.m.—the twilight hour. The bus symbolised budget travel, whisking me home for 2 rupees and a 40-minute journey.

It was a cold winter evening, and by 5:30 p.m., it was already dark outside. Back then, the buses in Delhi were pretty old and falling apart, and at night, it took much work to see the bus numbers. I needed to get off at the clock tower and then walk home. I was waiting at the bus stop, freezing, when I finally saw a bus going to the clock tower. I double-checked with the driver because the bus number was not visible. He assured me I was on the right bus, and I found a seat, ready for the ride home.

I was tired, and I fell asleep for a bit. When I woke up, it was 6:30 p.m., and I figured I hadn't missed my stop. Just to be sure, I asked the person sitting next to me, and he said, "Do not worry; the clock tower is the last stop for the bus." But as we kept driving, I started to feel lost. Everything outside was dark, and we kept passing bus stops I did not recognise at all. Time kept ticking by—it was 7:00 p.m., then 7:15 p.m., and I was starting to freak out. No mobile phones back then, so I couldn't just call my parents to let them know where I was. They must have been worried sick, was continuously in the back of my mind. I approached the driver again and asked when we'd reach the clock tower. He said, "Chill boy (I used to look 16 even in college), it's the last stop. You can't miss it." But I was starting to worry, especially since most people had exited the bus.

Finally, after what felt like forever, the bus stopped, and the driver announced that we were at the clock tower. I got off the bus, looked around, and realised this was NOT my clock tower. I couldn't believe it. I returned to the bus and told the driver, "This is not the right clock tower." Here is the worst part: by the end of the movie night, my wallet was empty. All my saved cash had gone into the movie ticket and some snacks. And yep, no dinner because that was way out of my budget, leaving me super hungry. Then the bus driver drops the bomb: we're at the "Clock Tower," but guess what? Wrong clock tower. He then tells me the one I meant to go to is a whopping four hours away. He pointed out that there are few clock towers in Delhi, and I should have been more specific.

So, there I was, no cash, no way to call my folks, stranded in an unknown place, and not in the mood to beg, especially since the market was closing. All I could think about was how to let my parents know I was ok (sort of) but stuck in the wrong spot, hoping they could rescue me. Back then, telephone booths were the go-to, but guess what? No money, no call. I've always been bold in asking for help. So, I tried my luck at a nearby shop, asking the owner if I could use the phone or if he could spare a rupee for the call. But this guy, rich in money but not in kindness, basically told me to hit the road, thinking I was just another scam story in his daily life.

Stuck without options, I needed to find a way to call home before even thinking about getting a taxi, which would cost me an arm and a leg—200 rupees one way! That's like losing four months of my pocket money for one blunder. So, making that call was crucial—I had to get my dad to pick me up instead of blowing all my savings on a cab ride home.

Out of options, I made my way to the nearest phone booth. The owner was not there, just the attendant. He must've seen the desperation in my eyes because, without a second thought, he told me not to worry and allowed me to make a call, saying he'd cover the cost himself. I quickly rang up my parents, who were relieved to hear I was safe. They told me to catch a taxi home and promised they'd pay the fare on arrival. They even said I wouldn't lose my pocket money over this—to them, choosing between their only son and 200 rupees was a no-brainer.

I got all choked up talking to them. In those days, privacy was not a top priority for anyone, so as I spilt my guts, the phone booth attendant overheard everything. After I hung up, he came over and, with the biggest heart, handed me 5 rupees he'd saved for his dinner. He said, "Brother, I am not rich, but take this to go back home. I will sleep better knowing I helped you out." He told me to remember him and that I could repay him if we ever crossed paths again. And if our paths never cross again, the best way to honour his kindness is by paying it forward and assisting someone in need.

With his help, I managed to catch the night bus back home. Years later, I returned to repay the kindness and more, but that attendant was nowhere to be found. I never got the chance to tell him, brother, that I had made it home safe. I may never have been able to return those 5 rupees, but I've kept my promise to him: to lend a helping hand to anyone in need. Because who knows? My assistance helps someone else reunite with their loved ones or reach somewhere.

Endnote Reflections

Time and again, I've faced dire situations, moments when everything seemed against me, maybe because I am the lucky one. Throughout my life, I've encountered moments where unseen forces seemed to emerge from the shadows, guiding me to the next chapter of my journey. But recalling the lesson from the story I shared, I realised all it takes is one bold step towards what I want, and somehow, miraculously, help always appears. It's like there's an invisible hand, you could call it fate or a higher power, that steps in when I need it most. And believe me, it always has. Therefore, don't be discouraged by life's challenging situations, as help is coming.

Notes

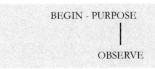
Story 27

Cut Off That Dead Leaf

We moved from a compact 2-bedroom apartment to a more spacious 4-bed house a few years ago. In the move, we filled over 25 boxes, ending up in our garage. Gradually, as we settled in, we unpacked these boxes, distributing our belongings throughout the new space thereby decluttering the garage. Initially, we thought of repurposing this extra space into something meaningful. As time passed, the garage again became a storage area, accumulating broken and unused items alongside boxes filled with things we thought might one day prove useful. Yet, 'one day' never arrived, and the garage became cluttered with obsolete items, effectively wasting valuable space.

I committed to routine clean-ups, recognising the need for order and utility, ensuring the space remained dry and free from potential decay. The turning point came when I acknowledged that the clutter consumed my time and energy and served no real purpose. Despite the costs, I purged the garage of all non-essential items, reclaiming the wasted space. With this cleanup, I chose to keep this area away from returning to a repository for discarded and unused items. I transformed, renovating the space into a functional office. It gave me additional space in my home and increased the value of my investments over time.

Our lives can also become burdened with what Ishu calls 'dead leaf': obsolete habits, unfulfilling relationships, and old beliefs that no longer contribute positively to our existence. These lifeless elements become like the clutter we mindlessly store away — they take up valuable mental and emotional space without providing any real benefits. It is crucial to assess these areas of our lives periodically. It involves a critical review and necessary updates or eliminations of these outdated habits, relationships, and beliefs, ensuring they align with current times. If they do not add value, they should be let go, much like discarding broken and unused items from a cluttered garage.

Failure to address these issues means we're essentially hoarding unnecessary burdens, draining our energy and time — resources that you could spent on a more productive area. Just as a clean, organised garage serves a better purpose, a life free of unnecessary 'dead weight' is more streamlined, energetic, and open to new opportunities and growth.

Endnote Reflections

- Just as you might periodically clean out your garage to prevent it from becoming overwhelmed with clutter, regularly observe and examine your life for habits, relationships, and commitments that no longer serve your best interest.

- Learn to let go of things that no longer serve you, much like how you would decide to dispose of or donate unused items in your garage.

- Just as you repurpose space for better use, view free time in your life as an opportunity for growth and new beginnings.

- Prevent old patterns from reasserting themselves. Just as you'd resist the temptation to fill an empty garage with new clutter, resist the urge to slip back into old, unproductive habits.

The New Kitchen Table

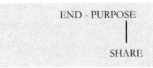

Story 28

Share Or,
Not To Share

If there's one lesson to take from a devoted and selfless nursery teacher like my wife, it's the importance of 'The Art of Sharing.' One morning, she eloquently explained 'The Art of Sharing ' to us at the kitchen table, illustrating it through the morning dew on the grass, which sparkled like diamonds under the sun's rays. She described how the sun doesn't lose anything by generously giving its light, yet the dewdrops gain everything from its presence. Similarly, when she selflessly shares knowledge and love, she helps kids to grow and prosper. While she may not immediately gain from this act of giving, she does contribute to kids' collective growth and enrichment.

She emphasised that to achieve selfless sharing, one must develop a service-oriented attitude and maintain calmness in character. Giving selflessly to others comes from a genuine desire to serve them without expecting anything in return. This aligns with what the PURPOSE scale illustrates: progressing from serving others to achieving a state of serenity and ultimately reaching the pinnacle of selfless sharing.

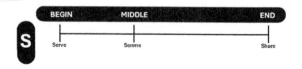

28.1 PURPOSE Scale - 'S'

"In tender soil, we plant with hope,
intentions pure and grand,
Nurture with love and grow dreams
So vast under life's demanding hand.

Through storms and sun, we care;
In gratitude, we must stand,
Harvesting hope from seeds once sown,
In heart's sacred land."

Endnote Reflections

Drawing from her wisdom, here are her insightful tips:

- **Practice Empathy and Active Listening**—By actively listening to others, you can deeply understand their needs and perspectives. Just as the analogy illustrates the selfless nature of sharing, you can better understand what someone needs and how best to support their growth and well-being by genuinely listening to them. This practice builds a strong foundation for selfless sharing, as it shifts focus from personal gains to the enrichment of others.

- **Cultivate Gratitude and Generosity**—Regularly reflect on what you are thankful for and act on these feelings by giving to others without expecting anything. By developing a habit of gratitude and generosity, you will appreciate your blessings and become more inclined to share selflessly, enhancing collective well-being.

Notes

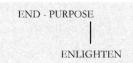
Story 29

Create Some Magic Moments, Not Numbers

One night at the kitchen table, Ishu asked, "Dad, what's an enlightened person?" He caught something on YouTube and needed help understanding it. Many people have different answers to what 'enlightened person' means, which an adult can follow. But what about breaking it down for a kid like Ishu? That's a different game altogether. My definition of an enlightened individual for him was "One who can experience and create magic moments in life." Anyone who understands how to bring those small and big moments genuinely grasps life's essence and is enlightened.

Sure, you might debate whether what I said to him is correct, pointing out all kinds of issues. But I explained to him this way because I wanted him to get one thing straight

– to become enlightened does not mean you have to spend your whole life searching for it—no need to follow a monk into the wild or spend hours in meditation classes to discover enlightenment. Just go out there, bring a magical moment into someone's life, and show gratitude to those who've done the same for you.

"The accurate measure of your knowledge lies in your ability to explain it to a child; this is the route to mastery and genuine insight."

Naturally, he hit me with a classic kid follow-up, "Am I enlightened?" Stick around, and I will share a story from when he was six, and you can decide for yourself.

One morning, while having breakfast at the kitchen table, I decided to tell Ishu a story about three kids pointing to a showpiece in our home. I began, "There were once three kids who lived in a village. The first child always kept a hand over his eyes, promising to 'see no evil.' The second child kept his hands over his ears, vowing to 'hear no evil.' And the third always kept his hand over his mouth, pledging to 'speak no evil.'" I am sure you have heard this several times, so I will directly jump to the point where I finished the story, and I ended up describing, to my son, the commitment to their principles and how they became examples for others in their village of good.

After finishing the story, I looked at him, expecting him

to be impressed and inspired by the virtues of the three kids. Then, with a thoughtful expression, he replied, "Dad, it's a good story, but I think something is missing."

Surprised, I asked, "What do you think is missing?"

"Well, if a fourth child kept a hand on his forehead, symbolising 'think no evil,' then the other three wouldn't need to cover their eyes, ears, or mouth, and one thing they had to do was to follow their brother. We won't see, hear, or speak anything bad if we never think bad thoughts. It all starts with our thoughts, right?" Penny dropped for me. It was the magic moment he created for me. For me, this was a suggestion from an enlightened soul. Would you agree?

But Why? Why do many of us not notice the real moments that make up our lives? I blame maths and our obsession with numbers. Don't get me wrong, Maths is my favourite subject. It feels like everything is about numbers these days. In school, it is all about who got what score; everyone qualifies students' efforts by numerical values for ranking. Then, the whole comparing game kicks in, trying to find the best from the worst based on more numbers. However, these high scorers are not always successful in real life, proving that exams do not always capture natural talent. Some kids do not fit in the number game – they are the outliers who might succeed in ways a scorecard can't predict.

Some of these high scorers in real life tell the world that success equals money, another numbers game. Society puts you on the sidelines if you do not stack up, nudging everyone to chase more digits in their bank accounts to win.

The New Kitchen Table

But our life is more than just a number score, more than just what is in our wallet. Individuals who cherish magical moments gather more than mere numbers; they collect experiences. In contrast, those fixated solely on numerical values may miss the true essence of these magical moments. I refer to those who grasp this concept and value the intangible over the quantifiable as enlightened souls.

Create Some Magic Moments, Not Numbers

Notes

IV

DIPOLE : Examine

———————●———————

Story 30

I Just Kept Fixing The Gaps

In earlier stories, we explored the DIPOLE framework and examined the method to find patterns in the chaos of life. Furthermore, we touched on other frameworks, such as OPTIMISM, NEAT, and ADAPT, particularly within the LEARN context.

In this section, we will explore the EXAMINE step of the DIPOLE Cycle. There are two primary outcomes of EXAMINE. The first outcome of the EXAMINE process involves analysing intakes from the PREPARE stage to find the areas of further improvement in the current event. The second outcome is crucial for channelling the lessons into LEARN, where the insights are solidified and stored for the future. Essentially, 'EXAMINE' gauges the change from the beginning to the end of the current event, enabling us to analyse and extract valuable lessons for current and future purposes.

The New Kitchen Table

Examining life events can seem overwhelming for many of us, complicating the process of reflection during life's complexities. Often, when confronted with numerous daily tasks, our primary aim shifts to merely completing them, neglecting the importance of examination and learning from them. We find ourselves trapped in a cycle of repetition, mastering familiar tasks within our comfort zones. It leads to a life on autopilot mode, where change is another word. To bring change in our lives, we may temporarily escape through vacations, living in temporary happiness, wishing for a permanent holiday state. But once we return to our daily routine, the dream vanishes, and we revert to our default settings of autopilot living.

One reason we resist real change is our uncertainty about gaps. Awareness and analysis of these gaps could significantly improve our chances of successfully implementing and adopting change. It would help if there were a step-by-step process for understanding this.

I've developed a detailed, step-by-step process to identify gaps by analysing events, enabling you to implement the right changes for yourself. You do step-by-step YOGA. Don't worry; I will not ask you to walk on your head and do a headstand. That may be for some other day, but I will introduce you to **'YOGA – Your Outgrowth Gap Approach.'** YOGA is about observing life around you and finding the 'oops' moments – where things could have been better; using its nine simple steps, you tackle these gaps in a structured way, checking your efforts and emotions at every stage.

Endnote Reflections

The whole point of the EXAMINE is to spot these gaps between expected and actual outcomes in whatever you're doing—studies, personal or official—and then fix and learn from them. This way, you're continually improving by learning and implementing changes. Once you have learnt something, this learning is cycled back into the DIPOLE as future input.

So, what's the takeaway? Be observant, curious, and not afraid to mix and match what's already within you to examine the world around you.

Notes

Story 31

Nine They Are

YOGA: **Your Outgrowth Gap Approach** is a step-by-step approach designed to identify and bridge gaps in the EXAMINE step of the DIPOLE Cycle. You should see YOGA as a growth review procedure that encourages you to find and address the 'gaps' in your personal or professional life events during the PREPARE phase of DIPOLE. These gaps could represent misunderstandings, skills that need improvement, unfulfilled goals, or areas of life that lack balance or harmony.

The 'Your Outgrowth Gap Approach' implies a customised introspection in which you evaluate your current state, identify areas that require change or improvement (gaps), develop strategies to bridge these gaps, and learn in an active, self-guided process towards better self-awareness, growth, and, ultimately, transformation.

You can also apply this approach to various life events, including career development, personal relationships, mental and physical health, and lifelong learning. By adopting a 'YOGA' mindset, you will continuously assess and adapt your strategies to lead more fulfilled lives. The method advocates a cycle of examination, discovery, and positive change.

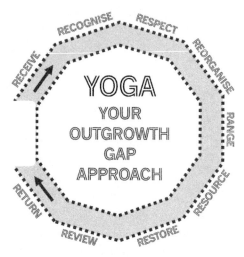

31.1 YOGA - Your Outgrowth Gap Approach

In essence, YOGA practice comprises nine integral steps, with each phase crucial and not to be omitted. The time allocated to each step may vary based on the event's simplicity or complexity, but the order and nature of the steps remain unchanged. This consistency ensures that the methodology is systematic and thorough regardless of the scenario.

The first step of the YOGA process is to receive current event details from the PREPARE phase when you have little clarity on areas that require improvement. It is followed by seven more steps, from recognising a gap to reviewing the solution and learning before YOGA returns the details (9th step) to PREPARE and LEARN. Iterative adjustments are made to an event, ensuring that the DIPOLE remains relevant and practical, finally leading to the best external outgrowth and learning. YOGA teaches us to continuously learn and improve with its steps, applying those lessons to future DIPOLE cycles. It's a cycle of reflecting, using, and getting better, setting us up for ongoing self-improvement and adapting to change.

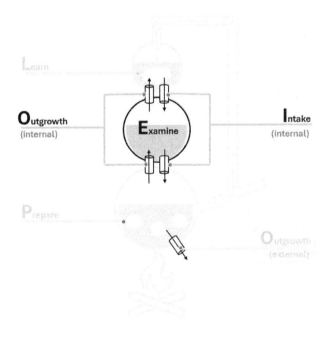

31.2 DIPOLE Cycle - EXAMINE

1. RECEIVE

Every batch of information sent from the PREPARE phase to the EXAMINE phase contains various elements: the initial intakes, detailed accounts of the PREPARE stage, and its results. On arrival, YOGA analyses this bundle of information to find issues and possible solutions to fix those issues.

At this juncture, it's common to feel overwhelmed by the volume and complexity of information received. For those not accustomed to managing such extensive and intricate information, there's a risk of confusion, potentially pushing you into a shock state. Hence, maintaining your composure is essential. Allow yourself adequate time to analyse and dissect the information.

During this step, your primary role is to gracefully accept the package without immediately diving into the depths of WISH (the Who, What, Where, When, Why, and How). It is the same as when accepting a delivery package from a courier without prior knowledge of its contents. Oblivious to whether it brings unwelcome news or an unexpected windfall, approach the information with an open mind. This initial receptiveness sets the stage for a more informed and structured follow-through in the subsequent steps of the YOGA.

2. RECOGNISE

One of the critical aspects of YOGA is recognising the need for a thorough analysis of the information. Allow yourself ample time to dissect this information before you try to move towards possible solutions.

This step is similar to finding the perfect spot to carefully unbox a package selecting a space that resonates with your comfort and readiness. It is your chance to understand the current circumstances. Your most critical attribute to embrace during this phase is curiosity—allow it to guide your exploration of the contents before you. Approach the information with the anticipation of learning something new, much like the excitement and wonder of unboxing a parcel. This curiosity will be your key to unlocking learning.

3. RESPECT

As the third step of the YOGA methodology, RESPECT stresses the necessity of approaching the received information with gratitude. This stage often leads to a range of emotions, primarily anxiety and hope, as one comes face to face with the nature and extent of the information at hand. Acknowledging and controlling these emotions allows you to absorb and reflect upon the information with composure and thoughtfulness. Anxiety and frustration may come as a natural reaction to unexpected challenges or complexities. Transforming this frustration into a thought of hope will give you a constructive force to move forward.

Gratitude plays a significant role. A grateful attitude toward receiving new insights, regardless of their immediate applicability or comfort, can significantly shift your approach to resolving gaps. Using the same example of unboxing the box, it shows respect while opening the box with anticipation and gratitude. Remember that each information inside the box may hold value for the next stage.

4. REORGANISE

REORGANISE centres on restructuring the information received into an understandable and actionable format. The objective here is to categorise each piece of information and find gaps, much like sorting through the contents of a cluttered parcel.

This reorganisation process requires a systematic approach. Begin by laying out all the pieces — the data, facts, feedback, and observations you have received — and then classify and group these elements based on their relevance, priority, and interconnections. This step may demand a degree of creativity and lateral thinking. The act of reorganising helps to transform the abstract or chaotic into structured and understandable elements. It's the process of arranging the contents of a parcel you have just opened; initially, the contents may seem unrelated, but as you begin to categorise and organise them, patterns emerge, and what was a confusion starts to make sense. You begin to see how individual components relate to each other.

By the end of this step, what was once a collection of pieces should start to form an understanding, laying the groundwork for a thorough analysis and identifying a range of possible solutions. Reorganising the information sets the stage for deeper insights and more strategic decision-making.

5. RANGE

RANGE explores and identifies potential solutions to enhance outgrowth and overall learning. It extends to both negative and positive discrepancies. Acknowledging both types of differences offers a holistic view of an event. It helps to find possible solutions and learn about their feasibility to improve your event's final result. This exploration is deeply rooted in optimism and resilience, two key attributes of YOGA philosophy. It is the step where you begin to discover how to use the contents of the delivered box.

6. RESOURCE

Each solution will require resources to implement it. RESOURCE provides exactly that, and it is about the strategic identification, allocation and utilisation of available resources for implementation. This step is crucial because it identifies practical actions and resources to support your idea. During this step, your planning and focus will be indispensable qualities. They fuel the drive to marshal the resources needed to effectively implement solutions, whether time, money, personnel, or materials. It's all about committing to the solution and ensuring you have considered everything. It helps to overcome obstacles and maintain momentum throughout the implementation. Let's say your box contains a birthday gift from a friend, a painting. Now, you are thinking of hanging it in your room, using resources like tape or a hammer and nail.

7. RESTORE

The central theme of RESTORE revolves around surprise and adaptability. During this step, creative thinking uncovers unforeseen challenges when reassessing your solution. It promotes a mindset that accepts these unexpected challenges. In our example, if you opt for the hammer and nail method, you might find you don't have the right size nail, preventing you from completing your task and possibly requiring a trip to the nearest store to buy the correct one.

8. REVIEW

The REVIEW step serves as a final checkpoint in the YOGA before transitioning the refined learning and solutions back to the PREPARE and LEARN. Here, you will ensure that all the areas of solution are covered. The goal is to affirm that the solution is complete, practical, sustainable, efficient, and replicable. You have finalised all the steps for utilising the box's contents.

9. RETURN

In the RETURN step of YOGA, we systematically compile and finalise information, readying it for the next cycle of PREPARE. This complete set of insights is also transferred to LEARN, which merges with our existing knowledge base. It enhances our collective wisdom and lays the groundwork for future actions and decisions. The 'Return' step is not merely an end but a bridge that connects the conclusions of one learning stage to the beginnings of another. It is when you have the instructions ready to be shared and acted upon on the items in the box.

Endnote Reflections

As we conclude our discussion on the YOGA model, we've explored the nine steps for your ongoing growth and learning. The upcoming stories will explore these steps with personal anecdotes, providing a detailed exploration of every aspect of the YOGA model.

Notes

Story 32

Your Council of Ministers, Living or Dead

Welcome to my grand nation, 'Life,' where I serve as Prime Minister. I 'Receive' a situation that needs resolution, which I accept as a challenge, and it is so unique that as the first person in my nation, I am the only one who can resolve it. But my governance is not solitary; my Council of Ministers guides me, voices both living and from the pages of history, ensuring that every decision is well-rounded and thoughtful.

Firstly, my Lower House, 'The Home,' is where the heart is, literally. It's the foundation, consisting of family and closest friends. They're the personal think tank, offering insights from the heart. They make sure the laws govern me and are based on love and practicality.

Then there's the Upper House, "Universe's Home," where my moral compass resides. It's like the ethical watchdog, ensuring my actions align with a higher purpose and the greater good.

Now, meet the Council of Ministers, each I have chosen for their unique contributions to the governance of the country 'Life':

- **Minister of Wisdom (Parent)** - These offer life-tested advice and unconditional support, grounding my decisions in experience and love.

- **Minister of Courage (Coach)** - The one who pushes me beyond the limits and teaches me resilience and perseverance through life's challenges.

- **Minister of Compassion (Best Friend)** - This person provides a shoulder to lean on and reminds me to be kind to others and myself.

- **Minister of Finance & Strategy (Mentor)** - A career and self-development guide who helped me navigate the personal and professional issues caused by gaps with foresight and planning.

- **Minister of History (Historical Figure, e.g., Mahatma Gandhi)** - This person lends perspective from the past and teaches patience and leadership.

- **Minister of Innovation (Inventor/Entrepreneur, e.g., Steve Jobs)** - Sparks creativity and encourages thinking outside the box, pushing the boundaries of what's possible.

- **Minister of Literature (Contemporary Authors)** - Through the power of storytelling, literature expands the imagination and provides escape and insight.

Your Council of Ministers, Living or Dead

- **Minister of Health (Personal Trainer or Doctor)** - This person monitors physical and mental well-being and reminds me that a healthy body houses a healthy mind.

- **Minister of Time & Balance (Philosophers)** - Ensures harmony between all aspects of life, advocating moderation and ethical living.

Together, this council guides my decisions on information or problems received, ensuring they are balanced, ethical, and forward-thinking. Each minister plays a crucial role, providing counsel from their expertise, and together, they form a comprehensive advisory board for me.

In life, it's critical to have a diverse, selfless council of your own who are here to ensure the PM (aka you) makes informed, compassionate, and wise decisions. So, as the young leader of your own life, think about who you'd appoint to your council and how long they will work with you. Choose wisely; these voices must guide you towards prosperity and peace.

Endnote Reflections

This step marks the beginning of receiving and assessing the event. This approach is not just about the initial identification and review; it extends to utilising a holistic set of tools and resources to address all aspects of the YOGA model, from end to end. Incorporating connections in life who serve as anchors, inspiring individuals through their books, drawing upon the wisdom of our parents, and analysing strategies used by historical figures in similar circumstances—all contribute to a more prosperous, better understanding of how to work with an event. These resources function as invaluable aids in constructing a foundation of knowledge, empowering you to tackle challenges with confidence and optimism. This approach enriches your perspective, providing diverse insights and strategies. It enables a deeper engagement with the YOGA model, encouraging a thorough exploration of each stage and ensuring a more effective resolution of gaps identified by YOGA.

Story 33

So, What If I Am Reinventing The Wheel?

Navigating the mysterious world of different personalities was like decoding Morse code, especially after a lifetime in an all-boys educational school. Imagine my family tree where attending boys-only or girls-only schools has become a family tradition. This way of learning didn't prepare me or my younger sister to handle all the different types of people and their unique ways of seeing things. I struggled to understand and engage with diverse personalities in the professional setup.

If I had followed in my ancestors' footsteps and done nothing about it, maybe I'd be just as underconfident with females as they were. Instead, I faced my problems directly and worked hard to change my situation. I could've blamed my genes and done nothing, but that wouldn't have gotten me anywhere and would have hindered my professional progress. The world isn't an all-boys or all-girls scenario; it's coexistent.

After all the effort, digging into the details, and spotting trends, I've seen it's just a straightforward principle. If someone had pointed this out to those before me, their lives might have changed. So, what's the finding for someone stepping into the chaos of adulting or navigating the corridors of complex people? It's simple: **'Be Genuine and Own Yourself.'** The real magic happens when you stop trying to fit into someone else's shoes but wear your own— no matter how quirky, different, or unconventional. That's the secret sauce to making friends and genuine connections.

Every day is a new adventure, a fresh start to experiment, to learn, and yes, sometimes recognise the fact that you may have to reinvent the wheel. Why not? If the wheel you're rolling is not getting you where you want to go, it may be time to sketch your blueprint. After all, being original is not just a choice—it's your superpower. I learnt that the best person you can be is yourself – it's the least crowded market. And yes, while it's scary to step out without the mask, it's also incredibly liberating.

Story 34

Missed Opportunities, A Bag of Lies

Life presents opportunities and mini-events that could lead us towards significant experiences and growth. In the '90s era of funky music, wild fashion, and the birth of internet chat rooms, I was navigating the confusion of being in secondary school, just like any other school kid. One of my friends kept nudging me, saying, "Hey, you have this knack for making computers do backflips. Why not try coding?" At that time, I made fun of my friend's recommendation and turned my back on it. If I had accepted the suggestion, it could have been my golden ticket to do something big. I decided to take a different path and jumped into Economics.

I progressed through a few years, many detours in my personal and educational life, and a couple of "What am I doing with my life?" moments to finally reconsider computer programming—the very thing I meant to do from the start. And guess what? It was like my life saying, "Told you so."

Like little paper aeroplanes, life will keep tossing these hints and opportunities at you. Some might fly straight, some might do loop-de-loops, but all of them have some message for you to work on. Respect these subtle messages and avoid dismissing them. Initially, they might feel daunting due to your lack of experience and knowledge. If you value these instances and allow time to comprehend them, you will likely discover answers to your problems more quickly. And yes, stop making excuses when you look back. "I made the right choice, I was being practical, blah blah blah..." But deep down, your mind says, "Come on, you know where you were wrong." It's ok to admit such mistakes and learn from them rather than lying to yourself and others and carrying this bag of lies on your shoulders for life. It's not about the lies we have told ourselves over the years which will make a difference, but it's all about the truths we're ready to face. Let's unpack those lies, examine them, and leave the bag behind. The travel ahead is much lighter without it, and who knows? You might find the path you meant to take.

So, my advice? Keep your eyes and mind open. Listen to those selfless anchors in your life and respect them, especially if they see something in you that you do not. Refrain from dismissing these mini opportunities. Finding those gaps in you is okay—your future self might thank you for it one day.

Story 35

Blank Canvas, Home Of The Dancing Dots

The difference between a once-in-a-generation painter and an ordinary painter lies in skill, vision, and perception. A master artist begins with a single dot and understands the power of each dot on his canvas. Each dot, each brush stroke, contributes to the final picture, which a master artist can see from the first one and reorganises those future dots to create a masterpiece. Similarly, we all are collections of many events, from moments of joy to sorrow, and each has its purpose in our story. Each contributes to vast, interconnected relationships that we will recognise over time. Our events, with all their joys and struggles, add depth to our story, emphasising the significance of every individual experience. They may seem random initially, but you will see what these events offer when you look at them collectively and reorganise them based on what you have learnt and experienced.

197

The New Kitchen Table

Each of us plays a part in this world, like a unique dot in harmony with countless others. Our paths, marked by our decisions and experiences, intersect and diverge from those of others, creating a distinctive pattern of existence. Those close to these events and observing them will understand future events intuitively. They begin to realise that the blank canvas is not just a void or a big gap but something filled with endless possibilities, an invitation to create and contribute. So, start each day fresh, free from the burdens of the past, with each moment providing a fresh opportunity to create something new every day.

Four Creatures

Four creatures lived in turbulent waters - a cunning Snake, a strong Octopus, a swift Fish, and a quick-witted Dragonfly. Each knew the other's strengths but often ridiculed their weaknesses, always trying to prove their superiority in the sea.

A massive whirlpool formed one fateful day, threatening to destroy their homes and underwater world. Survival was impossible unless they united, combining their unique abilities. With its sharp senses, the Snake detected changes in the water currents. The Octopus used its strong tentacles to create barriers against the swirling waters. The Fish, with its speed, gathered what was necessary. And the Dragonfly, flying above the water, coordinated their efforts and scouted for safe routes. As they worked together, a newfound respect was born. They realised that each one's strengths were crucial in overcoming the calamity.

This perspective encourages us to view everyone in our lives as interconnected. While each experience may appear distinct, bringing together the insights gained from each one empowers us to overcome any adversity.

Story 36

A Long Road Trip, A Life Lesson

I started on a memorable journey: a long road trip with my family from the southern reaches of England to the northernmost tips of Scotland, covering 2100 miles in 14 days. Unlike our typical short, planned vacations, this one was an unscripted adventure, except for the nine pre-decided stops. Carrying only the essentials, doing things we'd never imagined. Among the most daring was booking a stay in one of the remotest parts of Scotland, in the middle of nowhere within a 20-mile radius. For someone like me, who plans every detail, this was an experience in a parallel universe.

The journey unfolded in visits to unexpected, beautiful locations and encounters with kind souls. The weather, notoriously unpredictable in Scotland, surprisingly played a friendly host, gifting us 13 days out of 14 of perfect weather. Venturing into the remote Scottish landscape with endless mountains, hidden valleys, and grasslands tested our adventurous spirit.

But our trip to the remotest lodge in Scotland was an unforgettable adventure navigating the beautiful Scottish Highlands' roads. We were scared by the thought of driving through the inroads of the mountain range and grasslands, with no mobile or internet connections and limited food supplies, if something went wrong. One can easily imagine my situation when my wife suggested not to drive on this seemingly daunting journey. Despite my fear and uncertainty, I did not lose my confidence and adventurous spirit, pushing us into an experience that would assess our resilience, strengthen our bond, and leave us with unforgettable memories.

There I was, gripping the steering wheel, focused entirely on not turning our car into modern artwork against the picturesque backdrop. As we ventured, my mind raced with every possible worst-case scenario. "What if this wrong turn leads us off the map?" I thought, gripping the steering wheel tighter. "I have not even planned my will yet! And I never shared my endless list of passwords with my wife – the horror!"

Meanwhile, my wife turned into the saint of travellers, whispering prayers, probably hoping her spiritual GPS would guide us safely. Beside me, my wife tried to mask her worry with a reassuring smile, but her eyes were wide, screaming,

A Long Road Trip, A Life Lesson

"We're doomed!" Her thoughts were covered with practical concerns like, "Why did we not pack snacks? There's not even a single biscuit in here. What if we're stranded?" Meanwhile, she'd glance over, offering me a smile that was supposed to say, "We're fine," but screamed, "I can't believe you did not bring a bag of crisps!"

In the backseat, unaware of our internal panic, Ishu lived his best life. To him, this was no ordeal, eyes wide with excitement, not realising our distress signals. Every turn brought a new heart-in-mouth moment. We'd stop, snapping photos as if we could capture the sheer thrill and beauty of the moment, secretly praying our next stop would not be a headline in the Scottish news.

In the Highlands, the pinnacle of our trip was the stay at the remote lodge, a decision that initially filled us with apprehension. Remote in Scotland means isolation in the middle of nature's raw beauty, where roads can vanish into trails, and civilisation feels like a distant memory. Yet, what we feared most became the highlight of all our life trips. The lodge offered an experience like no other in the middle of nowhere. Surrounded by peaceful mountains and wildlife, hosted by the most gracious people, and treated to delicious vegan cuisine.

That night, under a full moon, in a cottage that seemed a world away from our everyday lives, I realised the true essence of travel. It's not about the planning or the certainty of the next steps but about the stories we gather, the people we meet, and the memories we create with our loved ones.

Ultimately, we develop a range of thoughts, experiences, and learnings full of optimism to take on bigger and bolder challenges in life.

Endnote Reflections

Here are the range of lessons from the trip:

- The destination matters, but the universe has a way of guiding you through the journey. Stay open to the path that unfolds.
- Recognize and utilise your companions' strengths. Success is a team effort dependent on each person's unique contributions.
- Cherish a partner who supports and balances you – they're your stability in life's unpredictable journey.
- Bring along someone younger, someone to care for and to share the joy and wonder of discovery.
- You will encounter many who are willing to assist and guide you on your path. Be open to receiving help.
- Tackle the activities that scare you the most; often, they lead to the most memorable and transformative experiences.
- Planning for fears is wise, yet sometimes, you will find the journey smoother than anticipated.
- Your body and health are your vehicles in life. Please keep them in top condition so they can navigate through challenging paths.
- On a long trip, the milestones genuinely matter, and finding joy during the journey towards them becomes essential.

A Long Road Trip, A Life Lesson

- Appreciate your achievements, and do not dwell on past mistakes. Learn from them and move forward with wisdom.

- Enjoy every moment, rain or shine. The slowest member sets the journey's pace, reminding you to move harmoniously with your companions.

I tell anyone wary of stepping out of their comfort zone to take the road less travelled. I love the uncertainty brought by a range of possibilities, for it is in the unknown that you write life's most beautiful pages. This road trip taught me more than how to navigate unmarked trails; it taught me about the joy of discovery, the strength in flexibility, and the unmatched beauty of life's unplanned moments. So, take that long road trip with your family when you can. It may change the way you see the world and yourself.

Notes

Story 37

Being Rebel Was Easy, Discipline Is What I Missed

Once again, I am revisiting the late '90s story of my failure in my final year. As you may recall, I had aced my second year in college, leading my class in Economics, a subject I chose in a burst of rebellion against my family and friends' wishes. It was my way of asserting my independence, of proving I could carve my path. But, as the final year approached, my world started to crumble. My lack of focus and discipline caught up with me, leading to my failing the final year and, consequently, missing out on an MBA program.

This phase of my life taught me a harsh lesson: being a rebel is easy; maintaining discipline is the real challenge. Even as the years passed, I did not quite master this lesson. I remained that undisciplined rebel, always searching and constantly questioning but not completing what I started, wasting opportunities, resources, and time.

The New Kitchen Table

It brings me to Ishu. Unlike me, he embodies a different kind of rebellion. Yes, he challenges norms and questions conventions, but he does so with a focus and discipline I never had at his age. As a teenager, he has already accomplished so much, not because he rebels without a cause but because he knows how to channel his rebellious energy productively. He sets goals, remains focused, and follows through with his commitments – qualities I admire.

Now, you might wonder where he got this. His discipline, focus, and approach to life are all gifts from his mother. My wife has been an example of patience and focus, qualities she cultivated over years of working with young children. She's the kind of person who, when she starts something, sees it through to the end, no matter the challenges. This single-minded dedication is what she has passed on to our son.

She's a rebel, too, but her rebellion is different. It's measured, purposeful, and, above all, disciplined. She challenges the status quo not by abandoning responsibilities but by fulfilling them and identifying the right resources to achieve what she wants. This approach to life and learning is what she has instilled in our son and in all the children she has taught over the years. The success of her students, their gratitude, and the lasting impact she has had on their lives are proof of her approach.

Rebellion is about more than rejecting what's given or expected. Actual rebellion leads to real change, and growth is about challenging yourself to improve and do better with

Being Rebel Was Easy, Discipline Is What I Missed
what you have. Setting your standards and diligently working to meet them is crucial. Finding your path is critical, but navigating it with purpose, focus, and perseverance is what truly matters. While it's ok to rebel against unjust norms or outdated traditions, your rebellion should be directed towards positive change in the world and within yourself. Be disciplined, focused on your goals, and patient in your journey. The most potent rebellions are not against others but against the lesser versions of themselves, urging them to rise, improve, and conquer challenges.

Notes

Story 38

Navigating Life Beyond Logic, Your Intuition Compass

Join me on a day in December 2010. This date sets the stage for the events that unfolded two days later. The story of that day begins with a family journey back from Mathura to Delhi. This outing was supposed to conclude a religious retreat but became a comedy of errors. Our car, filled with happy souls returning from a fantastic trip, suddenly became a race car on the highway. Our driver, perhaps mistaking the open road for the F1 track, decided speed limits were merely suggestions. As I sat in the back seat, my cautious side kicked in, voicing concerns about speed. My wife calmed me down and said, "He's a professional," Through her eyes, I saw, "We're all thinking it! But you said it."

Then, suddenly, a traffic cop appeared, who brought us

to a screeching halt. There we were, thinking we'd somehow teleported into a high-speed chase movie, only to be brought back to reality by a fine for speeding, watching my dad, a respected surgeon, trying to explain his way out of the ticket. He, who prides himself on a spotless record on the road, was now the family's outlaw, all thanks to our chauffeur. The silliness reached its highest point when my dad returned to the car with a ticket, sadly talking about his first-ever fine like a defeated hero. I, in the back, couldn't help but think there was a lesson here, but all I could focus on was the irony of the situation. We continued our journey home and were back home without any further scare. So, it was a day full of fun and a traffic issue, which I could have forgotten, but it kept playing. I saw a small gap that needed fixing before our next trip.

The next day, our car journey started towards Jaipur, the Pink City, where we looked for peace by visiting different holy places and going into the nearby mountains for a special ceremony. We heard about a bad car accident on the Delhi-Jaipur highway, the same route we drove on. The news said many people died in the car crash. This accident report lingered in my mind as we prepared to return to Delhi on the following day, adding to the ticket we got earlier. The sad event reminded me to enjoy every moment and be careful when on the road because it can bring unexpected challenges.

Despite the light-hearted start of our return journey, a sense of unease was there in me. Call it intuition or a sixth sense; something felt off. The previous day's tragic news stayed in my mind, mixing with the memory of the speeding fine and our driver's relentless pace. It was as if little breadcrumbs of caution were being dropped before me, urging me to pay attention and restore this gap with a possible safety solution.

My family did not notice I was worried, and I got comfortable for the trip. But I felt something terrible would happen if I did not take the proper steps. Because of this feeling, I asked the driver to stop to buy medicine. I just wanted us to slow down for a little while.

Back on the road, I felt even more worried. Everything seemed normal, but I told my wife and son to ensure their seatbelts were tight. They were confused, but it made me feel a bit better. I did not want to scare them, but I needed to keep everyone safe.

Then, it happened. Our car hit a truck head-on that was travelling on the wrong side of the road. The front of our car was like a cake on the floor, but the back part where we were sitting was intact. It was a miracle that we survived to tell this story. In the aftermath, as we stepped out of the wreckage, the reality of our narrow escape sank in. It was the same spot and type of accident reported earlier, but we were the survivors this time. When I reflect on those events, the warnings are clear: the speeding ticket, the unsettling news, and my unexplainable intuition. The universe had sent signals, nudging me to listen to my intuition and do something about it.

Endnote Reflections

This experience taught me the invaluable lesson of listening to that inner voice and recognising life's subtle signs. It reminds me that sometimes logic and reason do not hold all the answers; our instincts do. In navigating life, paying attention to these whispers can sometimes be the difference between being alive or dead.

Story 39

Character A Collection Of Blind Spots

My school switched from English to Hindi medium when I was in year one, thanks to the then government policy. Imagine, one day, you're learning apple, and the next, it's " सेब " (Hindi for apple). Just like that, my world flipped. What had I learnt? Life gives surprises; sometimes, these may be in a different language. Adaptability is not just a word in the dictionary; it's survival. Then, when I was 10, life took a darker turn. My mom battled depression, altering my young perspective. I learnt that even the strongest figures can struggle behind closed doors. It taught me compassion and that it's ok not to be ok.

Transitioning to secondary school, I faced another linguistic hurdle: back to the English medium. Maths, once my strength, became a foreign language. I saw a triangle, and my brain said "त्रिभुज". I failed badly in exams. Determined to reach my top spot, I learnt determination, the kind that makes you translate every word until 'triangle' looks and smells like a triangle. Hard work paid off, and I soon rubbed shoulders with the class toppers again. My status upgrade came with new friends. The learning? Success can be a magnet for new connections, but true friends stick around when the grades aren't sparkling.

Credit goes to my maths teacher, my school-time guardian angel. She saw potential in a lost boy and steered him back on track. Her belief in me gave me strength during my teenage turmoil. It's funny how life assigns you angels in disguise; mine just happened to be armed with algebra. At the same time, tragedy struck when a dear friend died in a bus accident. In an instant, youthful invincibility shattered. I learnt the harsh reality of life's fragility, a lesson no one's ever ready for. But life has a way of balancing your debits and credits. Engineering dreams crashed, and I landed in Economics – a field as alien to me as my computer textbooks in the 80's. I learnt resilience, the art of making the best out of plan B, and that sometimes, plan B stands for 'Better' plan. I topped my second year of college in Economics, a twist I did not see coming. If life were a poker game, this was the royal flush dealt from the bottom of the deck. It taught me that underestimation is the world's gift to the underestimated.

When a friend denied me a minor role, I created my stage by entering the same competition as a challenger. And the winner was? My play won, and I was the best actor. The lesson was that when doors slam, build your stage.

Then came the soul-crushing event, failing my final year. Rock Bottom has a basement. I never knew. I survived that as well; I learnt the most brutal but necessary lesson the hard way: getting up when life forgets you're down.

Thirty years later, life's been a combination of ups, downs, and many loops in between. Each blind spot and unexpected turn made me who I am. Life does not get easier; we get stronger, smarter, and, occasionally, luckier. Through the varied experiences of life, I've learnt invaluable lessons that have shaped my character. Each challenge and triumph has contributed to making me a strong **'Spring.'** Adaptability has been my first spring coil, teaching me that change is inevitable. Like a spring adjusting to pressure, I've learnt to navigate life's shifts and turns flexibly. I am not stiffening against change but moving with it, ready to stretch and adapt. Empathy, formed from witnessing the struggle, acts as another coil in the spring. It has taught me to understand and feel for others' experiences. Like in a compressed spring, empathy provides the gentle force needed to support and lift others and, in turn, us.

Perseverance, forged from overcoming failures, is a crucial coil. It has shown me that pushing through difficulties as spring expands leads to greater heights. Despite setbacks, persistence and the strength to continue moving upward are invaluable. Support from others has functioned as a reinforcing coil, highlighting the importance of community and guidance. Just as a spring relies on its structure for strength, we rely on those around us for support and direction.

The New Kitchen Table

Understanding life's fragility through loss and hardship has added depth to the spring, reminding me to appreciate every moment and bounce back with compassion and awareness after being compressed by life's weight. Resilience, learnt through repeated challenges, is the core of the spring's power. It teaches that after hitting the lowest point, just like a compressed spring, we have the inherent capacity to rise again, stronger and more prepared.

Endnote Reflections

These lessons have collectively built a spring strong enough to manage life's ups and downs. Navigating the peaks and troughs of life, your experiences, whether they stretch you thin or compress you down, are always preparing you for the upward leap. When life is tough, the same principles that stretch you will ensure a softer landing and provide the momentum for growth. And when you're at the bottom, every low point is an opportunity for a powerful comeback, with a new set of coils, stronger and more resilient than ever before.

Story 40

Never Compromise Character, There Is Always A Way

The story revolves around a critical moment in my professional life. I faced a significant ethical dilemma during a crucial client meeting. As someone responsible for meeting sales targets, I was under immense pressure to secure a high-stakes proposal to ensure a bonus for my team and me and avoid getting fired. Everything was going smoothly during the presentation, and the client was ready to move forward with our proposed solution.

During the discussion, I noticed a critical flaw in the client's plans and waited for the right opportunity to explore my concerns. Everything was going how we wanted when the CIO hit me with the million-pound question: "What's the one big mistake we're making?" Talk about being put on the spot! I felt like a contestant on "Who Wants to Be a Millionaire?" but without any lifelines on the last question. I had a choice: get clarity on my concerns and potentially sabotage the deal, or zip it and betray my moral compass. I weighed my options in those ten seconds, which felt more like ten years. Betray my ethics? No way. I have always played by the rules, even if sometimes it feels like my manual is from another planet. So, I took a deep breath, probably my most resounding ever, and asked about their oversight. The flaw was that they did not take buy-in from the business team, who were the ultimate users of the system; if unaddressed, it could lead to the failure in the adoption of the new system, leading to project failure, wasting time, effort, and resources for the client.

Despite the icy glares from my team (I swear, if looks could shoot, every cell of my body would have been on the wall), I stood by my decision. I mean, who wants to be the architect of a multi-million-pound disaster? Not me, despite my apparent love for high-stakes drama.

Two weeks later, while I was hanging by a thread in the company, what do you know? The CIO sent me an appreciation email and marked my leadership team. Honesty saved the day and secured a more significant, better project from my client as I was transparent with them. I had to start unpacking my bags because I was convinced that my bosses were about to parcel me to a monastery. To all my budding professional friends, please stick to your guns, even when it feels like you're the lone ranger. Integrity might make you the odd one out temporarily, but it'll earn you respect and trust in the long run. Plus, let us be honest: nothing beats the feeling of proving a room full of doubters wrong. It's the stuff of workplace legends.

Endnote Reflections

Henry and the Gold Coin

Once upon a time, a farmer named Henry lived in a small village. Henry was a hardworking farmer who spent his days tending to his crops and animals. Henry found a shiny gold coin one sunny afternoon while digging in his back garden. He had never seen anything so valuable in his life. Overwhelmed with joy, Henry decided to hide the coin. He chose a particular spot in his garden, buried the coin, and marked the place with a small stone. Every day and night, Henry checked the spot to ensure the coin was safe.

He became so consumed with protecting his gold coin that he neglected his farm. He stopped planting new seeds and taking care of his animals. His once flourishing farm began to wither, and his animals grew thin. But Henry's mind was only on the gold coin. He thought, "This coin is my only treasure. I am rich because of it."

Neighbours in the village started to notice the change. "Henry," they would say, "why have you stopped caring for your farm?" But Henry just shook his head and returned to guarding his hidden treasure, which no one knew about. Years passed, and the farm continued to decline. Henry spent all his time sitting by the small stone, never moving far from his precious coin. One day, his father visited Henry. Seeing the state of the farm and the obsession in Henry's eyes, which no one knew about, he asked, "Henry, what is going on? You have always worked hard. But now your farm is in a complete mess.

"Can I help you in any way?" Henry, trusting his father, told him about the gold coin he had discovered in his back garden. Father said, "You have a gold coin, but what good is it doing you? If you had spent this time working on your farm, you could have had a field full of gold coins and more. Protecting and worrying about that one coin made you lose everything in life."

Henry was stunned by his father's response. After a lengthy discussion, he finally realised that he had lost much more in his effort to protect his single coin. He had lost the chance to grow his farm, earn wealth, and enjoy life. From that day on, Henry changed. He started working on his farm again, planting seeds and caring for his animals. In time, the farm prospered, and Henry earned many more gold coins, far more than the one he had hidden in the ground.

This story of Henry and the gold coin is much like how many of us treat our jobs. We hold onto one job so tightly, afraid to lose it, that we miss out on other opportunities. We become so focused on protecting what we have that we forget to grow, take risks, and explore new possibilities. Just like Henry, we could achieve much more by working hard and looking beyond what we currently have. You do not have to compromise with your character to achieve something better. Encourage yourself to take calculated risks, strive for growth, take care of people that matter in your life and not let the comfort of the familiar hold you back from potentially more incredible successes.

Never Compromise Character, There Is Always a Way

Notes

V

DIPOLE : Explain

Story 41

Cutting The Air,
Stitching The Water

Imagine being ten years old again. But this is not about carefree days, playing catch in the yard, or worrying over which cartoon to watch. It is about being ten and feeling like the world's weight is on your shoulders. It is about me, a decade into life, navigating a storm not meant for a paper boat. Every morning was a roll of the dice, a question always hanging in the air: "What today?" At an age when most kids are learning to multiply, I was learning to manage a household dealing with deep depression. My mom, the heart of our family, was fighting her own battle, which drained the light out of our home and left all of us in darkness.

I walked through life with a mask I could fear at age 10. My father, a surgeon, was our only strength, tirelessly working to keep us afloat; his dedication was both inspiring and a reminder of the struggle at home. Each day was a balancing act: schoolwork, which seemed trivial compared to the real lessons life was throwing at my sisters and me; caring for my younger sisters, trying to shield them from what was happening at home; and the constant worry about my mom. Would she be ok today? Would she find some happiness with what she has, or would the day end in tears?

As for friends? They were like birds flying, and I couldn't reach them. Their laughter and carefree days starkly contrasted the tightrope I walked daily. I watched from the sidelines, an old soul in a young body, unable to share my world's reality for fear of the stigma. Every question from my mom was a test of my growing wisdom. I carefully weighed each answer. I was her confidant, her pillar, a role too prominent for my young soft shoulders, yet one I accepted because she wanted it that way.

I was cutting the noise at home and trying to make things seem normal when nothing was. It was about keeping our family intact, even when the connections were losing strength daily. But when you are pushed into the deep end – you learn as you go. The challenges, the responsibilities, and the fears changed me, teaching me an understanding of human psychology far beyond my age. These lessons became my armour, my guiding light through dark times.

This phase of my life, marked by battles and burdens no child should know, was also filled with invaluable lessons. When I look back on my past and use the methods, frameworks, techniques, and cycles I have described earlier in the book, I understand that that phase of my life taught me about the strength of the human spirit, the power of hope, and the unbreakable bond of family. It showed me that sometimes, being brave means standing up daily and facing the world, even when every part of you wants to hide. It is all about trying to create balance in life, and someone or something will come to your rescue no matter the size of the challenges you face.

Endnote Reflections

You may be reading this book for one reason or another, but did you expect this book to exist and come your way? Similarly, you will get lots of cues and support from your universe. But if, for whatever reason, you feel that you still have not found any support, maybe try my YOGA method to see where things are not working for you; maybe use the OPTIMISM Matrix to find what you can do with what you have in abundance which others may love to have from you and give you in return what they have. You could use NEAT Relationship Towers to understand connections in life. But do not mourn or cry; recall my dad's words, "If crying helps, let us all sit and cry."

So, to any beautiful soul reading this, know that your struggles, fears, and sacrifices do not go unnoticed. They shape you, strengthen you, and prepare you for a future where you can guide others lost in the fog.

Notes

Story 42

Hijacked By Work, Kidnapped By Masters

Everyone admires heroes. We aspire to perform extraordinary tasks as heroes do. For many of us during childhood, our superheroes are our parents. In my case, it was my dad, and no explanation is needed. But imagine a world where your hero, your dad, is there but not quite there. It was my reality, observing my father from the front-row seat of life, but it felt more like watching a movie where the hero was always on the brink, constantly battling, never resting.

My father stood tall and strong in all his hardships. A surgeon not by mere profession but by calling, he dedicated his life to serving the humanity that flowed through the government hospital doors. His days weren't measured in hours but in lives touched, saved, and transformed. My father, the first doctor from his village, became a lifeline, not just for us but for countless others who knew nothing of his struggles and sacrifices at home.

Hijacked by his work, he was constantly dealing with medical emergencies. We were proud but puzzled, always wondering why his presence and love were more for his patients and why his patients saw more of him than we did. We did not understand the weight of the invisible crown he wore, one forged from the relentless demands of his profession and the silent battles he fought within the walls of our home. The irony was stark – a man who fixed bones and healed suffering but a healer who couldn't cure his own household's aches. Our reality was that his work consumed him. It meant birthdays missed, school events unattended, and childhood milestones acknowledged with a nod rather than a celebration. From a tender age, it meant understanding that the man we called father was, first and foremost, a doctor to the world.

My father's relentless work ethic, commitment to his patients, and determination to provide for us painted a complex portrait of a man torn between two worlds. As I grew, so did my understanding. The man who seemed hijacked by his work was fighting a war on many fronts: ensuring our future, battling societal judgments, and navigating the dirty waters of professional politics. All while being the pillar for a family teetering on the edge of societal scrutiny.

This part of my life taught me the harsh truths of responsibility and the delicate balance of life's priorities. It showed me that being hijacked by work is not a choice but a condition often thrust upon those who dare to dream for themselves and those they love.

So, as you walk through your life, remember the story of my dad, who gave all, not only because he had to but also because he chose to, for the love of a family, for the unspoken promise of a better life. And know that when work tries to hijack your essence, think where your true north lies and steer your ship back home to where the heart truly belongs.

Typically, in childhood, each thread represents a different aspect of life – joy, discovery, and play. But these threads were interconnected for me with responsibility far beyond my years. I was not just a child; I was a confidant, a counsellor, a caretaker – kidnapped by the masters, my parents, each battling their demons.

On one side, there was my mother, her spirit shadowed by depression. A fragile and formidable figure, her world was one of endless questions, doubts, and fears only I could manage. I was a guide for someone who once guided me, trying to understand questions that could puzzle even the wise, trying to comfort her when I was looking for some of my own. It was my reality, a role reversal that no child is ever prepared for.

On the other side was my father, the surgeon, the provider, and the unintentional absentee. His demands were different – not of care, but of understanding, of stepping into shoes too big for my young feet. He shared not just the triumphs of his profession but its burdens, too. His professional world was challenging to navigate, and he expected me to be his guide on many occasions, deciphering the complexities of conflicts for him, office politics, and ethical dilemmas.

This dual role of being kidnapped by my masters was overwhelming. By day, I was a student, a brother, a friend – roles expected of a child. But by night, I transformed into a psychologist without a degree, a strategist without a plan, a confidant without a choice. I lived a dual life – one foot in the playground, the other in the battleground. But this kidnapping forced maturity; it sculpted me. It taught me to stay strong when times are tough. These lessons became the foundation of my character.

It taught me about the fragility of life and the strength of the human spirit. It showed me that family, in all its flawed beauty, is where we learn our most challenging lessons. It made me realise that we can find strength in our struggles and wisdom in our wounds. And so, to those who feel they are being kidnapped by their circumstances, by the demands of those they love, know this: It is not about your freedom but the shaping of your character. These trials and demands are burdens and blessings in disguise, teaching you lessons that classrooms and textbooks cannot. Accept the role, understand, and work on these challenges, and the child kidnapped by the master today becomes the master of not only their destiny but many others. The wisdom gained from the trials of youth can guide you through the complexities of adulthood. Every demand has a lesson; there's a chance to grow in every challenge. Over the years, my life partner and I have conveyed this to our son during countless discussions at the kitchen table.

Reflecting on my childhood, I realised it taught me to prioritise family over work. I inherited a strong work ethic and a deep sense of duty from my father. Observing him constantly consumed by his job taught me the importance of having a balance in life. I saw firsthand how a career could overshadow family time and personal well-being, whether noble or essential. It has led me to make tough decisions in my professional life, such as declining to accept work that consumes me and threatens to disrupt my family balance. I've learnt that no job is worth sacrificing precious family moments and mental health. This decision-making process made me understand that while careers are meaningful, they should not come at the expense of family and personal happiness.

From my mother, I learnt the importance of emotional support. Her battles with mental health issues were a significant part of my upbringing and taught me the importance of being there for loved ones when they need you the most. These experiences have shaped my approach to relationships and family life, emphasising support, communication, and compassion.

Endnote Reflections

To someone like you, navigating your challenges and difficulties now shapes you in ways you might not realise.

The New Kitchen Table

They're teaching you strength, empathy, and the value of prioritising what truly matters. Setting boundaries is ok, especially when balancing work and personal life. It's essential to know that success is not solely defined by professional achievements but also by the happiness and well-being of you and your loved ones. Your challenges, no matter which phase of your life, can be a source of strength and wisdom as you move into the future, helping you to make informed decisions that align with your values and priorities. Carry these lessons forward, using them to guide your choices and shape a future where family and personal well-being are at the forefront.

Story 43

Gold Is Gold,
Sold Or Unsold

One of my best friends and I met as strangers in the UK, both of us a long way from home, initially connected by circumstance rather than choice. Our days were filled with the usual challenges of adapting to a new country. These very challenges drew us closer together. We were colleagues working for the same company, but our relationship quickly evolved beyond the confines of office walls. Our friendship was solidified by shared experiences, from navigating the complexities of a new culture to celebrating small victories like mastering the local dialect or finding a taste of home in a foreign land. These experiences, while seemingly minor, were monumental for us, creating a solid and sincere bond.

Our weekends were spent exploring, sometimes with a

clear destination, other times just wandering the streets, travelling in local buses, and letting curiosity be our guide. We shared stories of our families, our aspirations, and the lives we left behind. In those moments, we weren't just friends; we were brothers, each other's family in a land where everything else was unfamiliar. The elan between us grew naturally. We became each other's confidants and best friends, sharing joys, fears, and insecurities. Our conversations could leap from light-hearted banter to deep, philosophical discussions without missing a beat.

Financial hardships, personal challenges, and usual ups and downs were all faced together. When I encountered financial difficulties, he came to my rescue without a second thought. Such acts of kindness and selflessness were the foundation on which our friendship stood. It was not about keeping score but about unconditionally being there for each other and being an anchor. We lived with the comfort of knowing that no matter what, we had each other's backs. It was the essence of our friendship, a genuine connection filled with mutual respect and admiration.

The surprise on my 40th birthday remains one of the most surprising chapters of our friendship. Amid my friend's personal tragedies back in India, he found the strength and love to board a flight to meet me in the UK. The moment he stood at my doorstep, bouquet and gifts in hand, was surreal. Here was a man who, despite his burdens, had traversed thousands of miles to bring me a smile. That gesture summarised everything for me about our love and friendship. The emotional weight of that surprise was magnified when, amidst the celebration, he shared the burdens he'd been carrying. His voice, usually full of life, was sad as he spoke of family losses and personal health battles. But even in sharing, he maintained positivity as if to spare me from his pain.

However, nothing could have prepared me for the phone call months later when he revealed his stage four cancer diagnosis. Soon, we started talking to each other for hours every day. The conversations were heart-wrenching, a mix of disbelief, shared memories, and fears. We spoke of everything and nothing, trying to bridge the physical distance with words, clinging to the hope that, somehow, this was just another hurdle we'd overcome together.

Over the next two years, our conversations became his lifeline. We discussed every conceivable topic, from mundane daily updates to life reflections. Despite the grim reality of his condition, he seldom blamed his fate. Instead, he focused on the present, enjoying each moment, each conversation. He faced his diagnosis with bravery that inspired me, teaching me about the true essence of being alive. Our talks were not just a distraction for him from his pain and worries but became sessions of mutual growth. He never lost his sense of humour nor his will to fight. Even as his physical strength deteriorated, his spirit remained high.

His battle with cancer, though harrowing, never defined our conversations. They were filled with laughter, tears, and sometimes silence, as if acknowledging the sacredness of our connection. In those moments, we weren't just friends battling a disease; we were two souls connected by an unbreakable bond. Our physical journey ended long back, but the lessons I learnt with him still shape my conversations with my family around 'The Kitchen Table.'

Endnote Reflections

True friendship shines like priceless gold where value is measured by moments of selfless love and support. It is a bond where distance won't matter, and hardship will become another word. In life, there will be times when no existing frameworks, models, or methods appear effective. Yet, the journey must continue, stepping bravely into the unknown. I have consistently taken that leap of faith, guided by my experiences and eager to assist others as best as I can. I value those who have stood by my side, for they have enriched my life with golden insights, whether those nuggets are sold or remain unsold.

Gold Is Gold, Sold Or Unsold

Notes

VI

DIPOLE : Message

Story 44: Be The Lantern, Not Smoke, In The Fog

Dear Son,

We have grown up hearing that we shouldn't trust strangers. The world becomes untrustworthy because we refuse to trust strangers. The fact is that every friend and every loved one in your life started as a stranger, even us as parents for you.

The experiences I have written about here are mine alone – they're not better or worse than anyone else's, simply different. But sharing them was worth it if my stories can help you see a little clearer, feel a little lighter, or smile a little brighter. Around 'The Kitchen Table,' I have shared pieces of my life with you for many years. Not because I think I've got it all figured out but because there are some valuable lessons in my life story that you can use to build your own life. Life's been a wild ride with its ups and downs, and through it, I have learnt a thing or two, which I have shared. You see, every person we meet, every smile we share, and every challenge we face teaches us something. And I want you to know that it's ok. It's ok to be confused, make mistakes, and sometimes feel lost. That's part of growing up.

Life will present you with a variety of challenges. You can either cry about your misfortune or work on it to learn those things that can create miracles for others in the future. Being a guiding light for someone does not mean you have to be perfect or have all the answers. It just means being there, being kind, and being yourself. Even the smallest act of kindness from you can make a massive difference to someone who's struggling.

I am not just writing to you as a father; I am talking to you as someone who cares, maybe a coach, a guide, a friend, or a well-wisher. I have been where you are and want you to know you are not alone. You have so much potential, so much to give, and so much to explore. Life will not always be easy, but with each step you take, you become stronger, smarter, and more capable.

"Be Kind,
Be Curious,
Be Brave."

Hold your head high; you can always rely on me even if you feel alone. I will always be cheering you on. Why? Because you have always been my selfless anchor. I am humbled, and I promise to be your lifelong anchor, too.

Love You My Life

Story 45: The Power Of Pause, Kitchen Table Stories

Dear Mum and Dad,

In our busy lives, filled with deadlines, activities, and constant digital distractions, it is easy to forget the powerful lessons around the kitchen table. Our house has been my learning centre, where you have shared your life lessons with me. Like a library filled with stories and a laboratory with experiments, our home—and especially our kitchen table—is where real learning shaped my mind.

Those quiet moments at the end of the day when we sit down around the table, you acted not just as parents but as guides, coaches, guardians, and friends. And you, as my parents, have wisely performed a sacred duty: to nurture, protect, and prepare me for life.

In the rush of daily life, you made sure to pause, share your stories, listen to mine, laugh together, address my fears, and celebrate my successes. So, no matter how busy life gets, please make time for these daily moments for me. Let our kitchen table forever be a place of warmth, wisdom, and strong bonding.

Just Your Bundle Of Joy

Notes

Story 46: Beautiful Note
To Our Past

Dear Past,

Thank you for being the partner in our learning and giving us unforgettable memories to share. Your lessons have become the wisdom guiding us in the present and sculpting our future. My family would choose not to alter a shared moment if granted a wish. We would ask for the same loving relationships, family, loyal friends, and strangers again, who encouraged us to prioritise what truly matters—time with our loved ones. Each event you brought into our lives, each obstacle and triumph, has taught us invaluable lessons, crafting the stories we share today.

Thank you for the lessons, the memories so rare,
Guiding us with wisdom and shaping our future with care.
With the same loving family, the same stories told,
We would wish for no changes, for each moment has been gold.

If these words can inspire or comfort anyone, then every challenge I face and every victory I celebrate validates that our conversations today have been worth every moment.

With Respect & Gratitude,

Oh Lord! Dreams of stars I once held dear,
Now grounded, yet my purpose is clear.
Shade, I give to those in need,
Fruits I bear, from which hearts feed.

Seeds within my fruit, a future sown,
From rocky starts, a forest grows.
No longer do I regret my past,
For in my branches, dreams hold fast.

Though stars I touch not with my leaves,
In souls I touch, my dream achieves.
Past and future, in me, unite,
A story of my never-ending flight.

Story 47: Future Echoes, The Past Ahead

My Dear Future,

A seed from the heavens found itself wedged between rocks. Too small to escape their grasp, it waited patiently, gathering strength. Despite the passage of time, its situation remained unchanged. Then, a gust of wind dislodged the rocks, freeing the seed, only to cast it to the mountain's edge, trapped once again by stones immune to even wind's force.

Unexpectedly, this time, a bird spotted the seed, lifting it with the promise of freedom, yet fate twisted again, turning the seed into potential nourishment for the bird. The day's heat weakened the bird, causing it to drop the seed onto fertile ground. There, nourished and supported by soil, the seed sprouted in a few years and grew into a grand tree.

The seed, now a tree, reflected on its journey: originally intending to touch the stars, it had instead become a haven, providing shade and fruits for others. Each fruit, though beyond its enjoyment, carried the promise of new life inside it, a legacy of strength and growth. The tree realised it might not touch the stars but could become a pillar for others' dreams.

Your Sincere Present

Notes

VII

DIPOLE : Add On

My Sincere Gratitude To Authors

I offer my deepest gratitude to the below authors and their books. They have left a mark on my life, whether through the pages of their creations, online videos, or podcasts. Their stories, experiences, and wisdom have touched me immeasurably, continuously lighting my path.

- Aurelius, M. (2006). Meditations. Penguin UK.
- Bannerman, J. (2012). Genius!: deceptively simple ways to become instantly smarter. Harlow: Prentice Hall Life.
- Butler-Bowdon, T. (2014). Never too late to be great: the power of thinking long. London: Virgin Books.
- Byron, M.L. (2012). Live Your Dreams. Createspace Independent Pub.
- Cal Newport (2016). So good they can't ignore you: why skills trump passion in the quest for work you love. London: Piatkus Books.
- Carey, N. (2013). The epigenetics revolution: how modern biology is rewriting our understanding of genetics, disease, and inheritance. New York: Columbia University Press.
- Carnegie, A. (2018). Autobiography of Andrew Carnegie. New York: Snova.
- Carnegie, D. and Overdrive, I. (2010). How to Win Friends and Influence People. S.I.: Simon & Schuster.
- Clear, J. (2018). Atomic habits: tiny changes, remarkable results: an easy & proven way to build good habits & break bad ones. New York: Avery, An Imprint Of Penguin Random House.
- Collier, R. (2013). The Secret of the Ages. Merchant Books.
- Coyne, K.P. and Coyne, S.T. (2011). Brainsteering. Harper Collins.
- Dawson, R. (n.d.). Secrets of Power Negotiating.
- Dianna Daniels Booher (2011). Creating personal presence: look, talk, think, and act like a leader. San Francisco: Berrett-Koehler Publishers.
- Dr. Bob Rotella (2012). Your 15th Club. Simon and Schuster.
- Dyer, W.W. (2012). Change your thoughts, change your life: living the wisdom of the Tao. Carlsbad, Calif.: Hay House.
- Fisk, P. (2011). Creative genius: an innovation guide for business leaders, border crossers and game changers. Chichester: Capstone.
- Foer, J. (2011). Moonwalking with Einstein: the art and science of remembering everything. New York: Penguin Books.

The New Kitchen Table

- Gardner, A. (2012). Change Your Words, Change Your World. Hay House.
- Gilbert, E. (2016). Big Magic. Penguin Usa.
- Goggins, D. (2018). Can't hurt me: master your mind and defy the odds. United States: Lioncrest Publishing.
- Grant, A. (2023). Hidden Potential. Penguin.
- Gratton, L. (2014). The shift: the future of work is already here. London: William Collins.
- Greene, R. (1998). The 48 laws of power. London: Profile.
- Greene, R. (2010). The 33 Strategies Of War. Profile Books.
- Greene, R. (2013). Mastery. New York, New York: Penguin Books.
- Hallowell, E.M. (2011). Shine: using brain science to get the best from your people. Boston, Mass.: Harvard Business Review Press.
- Hamilton, D.R. (2010). It's the Thought That Counts. ReadHowYouWant.com.
- Héctor García, Francesc Miralles and Cleary, H. (2017). Ikigai: the Japanese secret to a long and happy life. London: Hutchinson.
- Hill, N. (2018). Think and Grow Rich. General Press.
- Hoover, T. (2010). Zen Culture. Thomas Hoover.
- Hoover, T. (2016). The Zen Experience. Nmd Books.
- Huang, T.M.A. (2010). The Complete I Ching: the Definitive Translation by Taoist Master Alfred Huang. Rochester: Inner Traditions International, Limited.
- Hyemin, Kim, C.-Y. and Lee, Y. (2018). The things you can see only when you slow down: how to be calm in a busy world. Uk: Penguin Life, An Imprint Of Penguin Books.
- John Paul Carinci (2018). The Power Of Being Different.
- Kahlil Gibran (2020). The prophet: timeless wisdom for modern life. London: Bluebird.
- Keller, G. and Papasan, J. (2013). The ONE Thing. Bard Press.
- Koch, R. (2016). LIVING THE 80/20 WAY: work less, worry less, succeed more, enjoy more...
- Kurzweil, R. (2014). How to create a mind: the secret of human thought revealed. London: Duckworth.
- Laozi and Mitchell, S. (1988). Tao te ching: a new English version. New York, N.Y.: Harper & Row.
- Lax, D.A. and Sebenius, J.K. (2006). 3-D negotiation: powerful tools to change the game in your most important deals. Boston, Mass.: Harvard Business School Press.
- Lipton, B.H. and (2015). The Biology of Belief. Hay House Publishing.
- Manning, H., Bodine, K. and Forrester (Firm (2012). Outside in: the power of putting customers at the center of your business. Boston: Houghton Mifflin Harcourt.

My Sincere Gratitude To Authors

- Manson, M. (2016). The subtle art of not giving a f**k: a counterintuitive approach to living a good life. New York: Harperone.
- Michalko, M. (2014). Thinkertoys: a handbook of creative-thinking techniques. Berkeley: Ten Speed Press.
- Morrell, M. and Capparell, S. (2012). Shackleton's way: leadership lessons from the great Antarctic explorer. London: Nicholas Brealey.
- Nafousi, R. (2022). Manifest. Chronicle Books.
- Newport, C. (2018). DEEP WORK: rules for focused success in a distracted world. Grand Central Publishing.
- Nhât Hanh, Thích and Kotler, A. (1995). Peace is every step: the path of mindfulness in everyday life. London: Rider.
- Nugent, K. (2010). Change, bring it on! a simple, workable framework for leading and managing successful business transformation. Oxford, U.K.: Infinite Ideas Ltd.
- Poundstone, W. (2011). Priceless: the myth of fair value (and how to take advantage of it). New York: Hill And Wang.
- Pressfield, S. (2002). The war of art: winning the inner creative battle. New York, Ny: Rugged Land.
- Roberta Chinsky Matuson (2011). Suddenly in Charge. Nicholas Brealey.
- Robinson, K. (2011). Out of our minds: learning to be creative. Oxford: Capstone.
- Robinson, K. and Aronica, L. (2010). The Element: how finding your passion changes everything. Camberwell, Vic.: Penguin.
- Seven (2010). Mind Strategies.
- Silva, J. (2022). Silva Mind Control Method. S.L.: Gallery Books.
- Sukhinder Singh Cassidy (2021). Choose Possibility. Pan Macmillan.
- Troward, T. (2020). Creative Process In The Individual. S.L.: Indoeuropeanpublishing Co.
- Tzu, S. (2012). The Art of War (The Classic Lionel Giles Translation). e-artnow.
- W. Timothy Gallwey (2010). The Inner Game of Tennis. Random House.
- Wattles, W.D. (2019). The science of getting rich. New York: Gildan Media Llc.
- Wheatley, M.J. (2010). Leadership and the new science: discovering order in a chaotic world. Great Britain]: Accessible Publishing Systems.
- Wiest, B. (2020). The mountain is you: transforming self-sabotage into self-mastery. Brooklyn, Ny: Thought Catalog Books.
- Zack, D. (). Networking for people who hate networking : a field guide for introverts, the overwhelmed, and the underconnected. San Francisco, [Alexandria, Va.]: Berrett-Koehler Pub.; ASTD Press.
- www.youtube.com. (n.d.). Official Alan Watts Org - YouTube. [online] Available at: https://www.youtube.com/@AlanWattsOrg [Accessed 28 Mar. 2024].

Index Of Topics

Printed in Great Britain
by Amazon

41848425R00145